Visual Merchandising

Laurence King Publishing

Visual Merchandising

Window and in-store displays for retail

Tony Morgan

LAURENCE KING

Published in 2008 by Laurence King
Publishing Ltd in association with the
University of the Arts: London College
of Fashion

Laurence King Publishing Ltd
361–373 City Road
London EC1V 1LR
Tel +44 20 7841 6900
Fax +44 20 7841 6910
Email: enquiries@laurenceking.co.uk
www.laurenceking.co.uk

A catalogue record for this book is
available from the British Library

ISBN 978 1 85669 539 8

Designed by Kerrie Powell

Printed in China

Page 2
A metallic window scheme entitled
"Mirror Mirror" attracts customers
with its reflective qualities at
Selfridges, London.

Contents

6   Preface

8   The History of
     Visual Merchandising

16   The Role of a
     Visual Merchandiser
19   The day-to-day role of a
     visual merchandiser
20   Training
21   Visual merchandising in a
     department store
24   Visual merchandising of
     chain stores
26   Visual merchandising of
     small retail outlets
27   Measuring success

28   Store Design
30   What is store design?
31   Why is store design important?
32   Who designs the store?
34   How does store design work?
36   Store study:
     Kurt Geiger

40   Windows
44   Getting to know your windows
50   Planning a window display
54   Themes and schemes
61   Budgeting
62   Props
68   Designing a window display
74   Store study:
     Lane Crawford
78   Color
84   Window prepping
86   Installing the window display
90   Lighting
92   Signage and graphics
98   Window calendar
102 Window standards
     and maintenance, and budget
104 Store study:
     Fortnum & Mason

108 In-store Visual Merchandising
112 Product adjacencies
114 Floor layouts
124 Store study:
     Atelier 1
126 Fixtures
138 Wall fixtures
142 Product handling
148 Store study:
     Flight 001
154 In-store displays and trend areas
158 Point of purchase and
     add-on sales
160 Clearance merchandise
161 Signage and tagging
168 Lighting
170 Ambience
172 Retail standards and
     maintenance, and budget
173 Virtual visual merchandising
176 Store study:
     Giorgio Armani

180 Mannequins
184 Sculpting
186 Purchasing mannequins
188 Dressing a mannequin
193 Securing a mannequin
194 Grouping mannequins
195 Maintenance

196 The Visual
     Merchandiser's Studio
200 The visual merchandiser's
     toolbox
201 Health and safety

202 Lighting chart
204 Glossary
205 Further reading
206 Index
208 Picture credits and
     acknowledgements

Preface

"It is your imagination that needs to be stimulated. Once that happens, the rest is easy. The merchandise is always the leader."

Joe Cotugno, OVP and Creative Director, Bloomingdale's

If you have ever stood outside a shop admiring the artistry of the window display, or been distracted by a sale item while passing though a department store, or paused to take in information from a store guide, then you have been sidetracked by visual merchandising. If you purchased as a result of stopping in your progress along the sidewalk or through a store, then you have succumbed to its supremacy.

For years, the creative individuals who made the stores of the world look appealing for retailers and their loyal customers were known as window dressers or display artists. Display teams had a unique and much-envied function in a store. Occasionally with generous budgets—and most definitely with a huge amount of talent—they mysteriously locked themselves away in studios or lurked behind the curtains of the windows and produced stunning, eye-catching works of art for the shopping community to admire.

During the 1980s, possibly because of a global recession and the threat of e-commerce from the Internet, store bosses suddenly questioned the quantities and abilities of these non-profit-making departments. As a result, they began to push the display artists in-store to cast a creative eye over the racks and rails of discounted merchandise; thus the visual merchandiser was born.

Rarely taken seriously at first because their new roles were unexplained, visual merchandisers were soon laying out departments complete with "sight-lines," "focal points," and "hot shops." A new retail vocabulary was born, and soon store interiors had as much sparkle as their windows. Today, visual merchandisers command respect, and are a much sought-after commodity in the retail world as they provide not only a service but also inspiration and commerciality. This book aims to enlighten and educate students and retailers in the workings of the world of the visual merchandiser. It covers both the art of the window display and in-store visual merchandising and looks at the tools that will help any would-be visual merchandiser succeed.

By using case studies and specially commissioned illustrative diagrams together with images of the best in window display and in-store interiors from around the world, this book aims to prove how effective visual merchandising will improve a store's brand image and inspire customers to spend.

Opposite
A mannequin reclining on a chaise longue lounges at the Rootstein showroom in New York. At a glance this realistic model looks almost human in appearance.

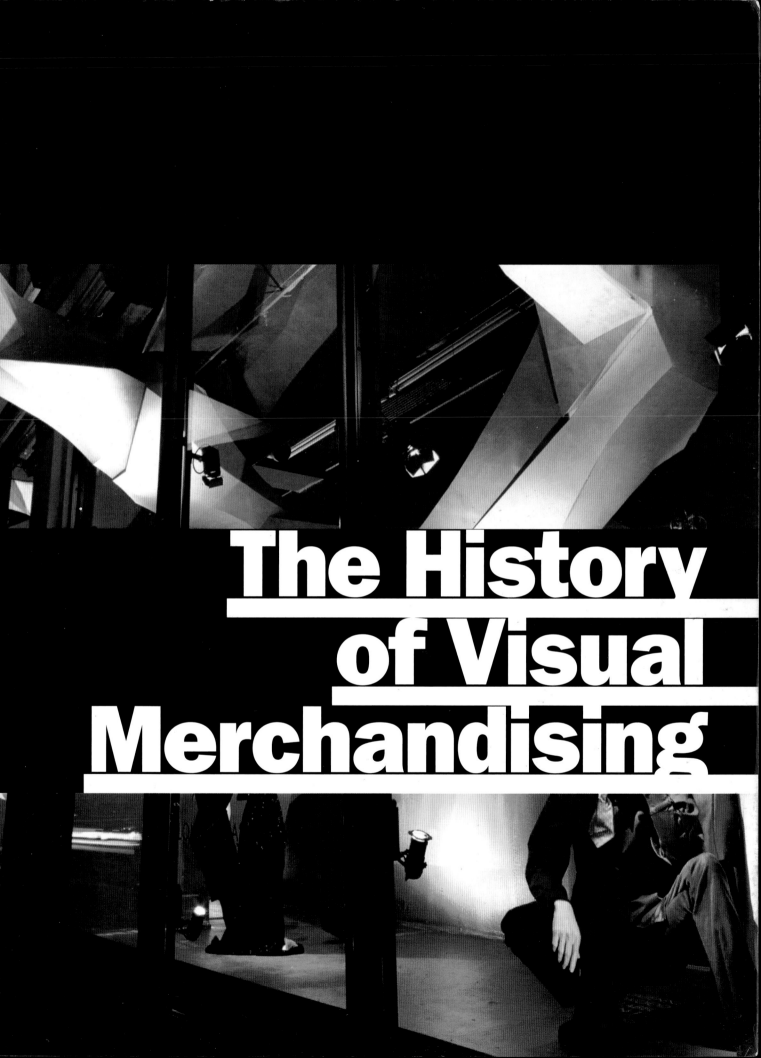

The History of Visual Merchandising

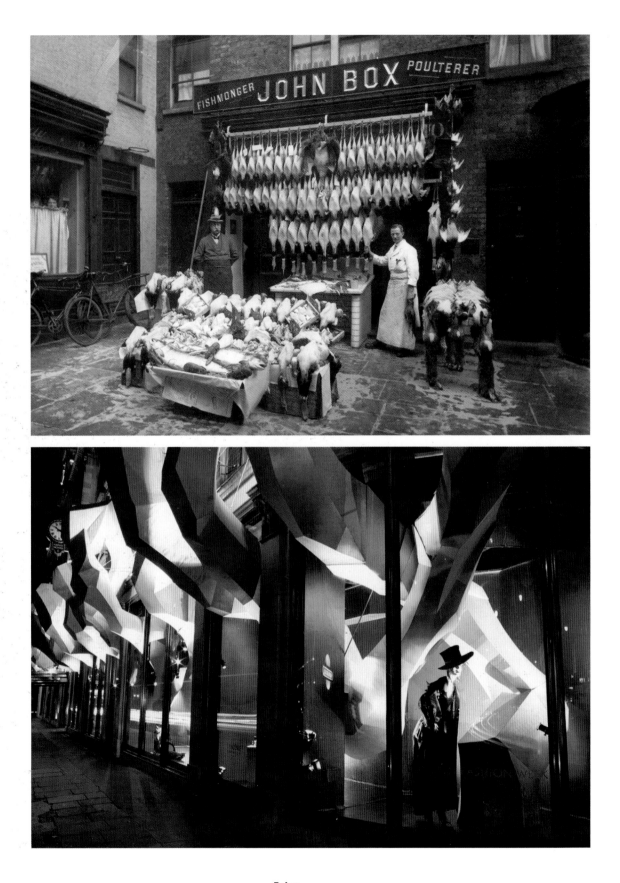

Above
Here the fish and poultry seller has created an artistic display of his wares, the design of which would not look out of place in the display lore of visual merchandisers today.

Below
In these attention-seeking, award-winning windows designed by Thomas Heatherwick for Harvey Nichols in London, the scheme explodes through the glass onto the exterior of the store.

The first shopkeepers tried to lure consumers into their stores either by ostentatiously exhibiting their names or by displaying products in their windows or on tables in the street, proving that they were open for business and proud of their produce.

To this day, butchers still fill their windows with fresh meat that serves both as a display to attract customers and also shows the cuts available for sale that day. Florists often not only pack their windows with the finest blooms, but trail them outside the store and onto the sidewalk to entice customers across the threshold using color and scent. Similarly, barbers will sometimes push a chair with an unsuspecting client up to the glass window in order to prove their skill and popularity.

With the advent of new technology in the 1840s that allowed the production of large panes of glass, department stores were perhaps responsible for taking the art of window display to a higher level, using their large windows as stages, some of them as theatrical as a Broadway show. Today, color, props, and atmospheric lighting on many occasions arrogantly overshadow the merchandise, as visual merchandising extends beyond its role of supporting the wares and becomes an art form, creating a statement or provoking a reaction. Stores like London's Harvey Nichols have collaborated with designers and artists to produce eye-catching schemes where the merchandise becomes part of an artistic work.

It is the department store, with its huge array of merchandise and vast amount of window space, that is the pioneer of the window display. A relatively recent phenomenon, it first began in France. Even there, however, for many years department stores existed only in the capital, Paris. It was Aristide Boucicaut who first had the idea of setting up this kind of

Above
Bon Marché department store in Paris in the late nineteenth century offered an impressive shopping experience for its customers through the grandeur of its architecture.

Below
A Selfridges window from 1920s London shows skill and imagination for its time, with its delicate display of handkerchiefs.

Above

The 1960s saw the creation of high-street ready-to-wear, and Mary Quant was one of the first designers to use the window of her London store in 1959 as a showcase for her collections, as well as to promote social trends.

store. He wanted to create a shop designed to sell all sorts of merchandise, but also wanted to attract crowds of people who could wander freely about in a little "town within the town." In 1852 Boucicaut opened the world's first department store: Le Bon Marché.

The concept of the department store then spread to the United States, where famous stores as we know them today first opened: Macy's in New York in 1858, Marshall Field's in Chicago in 1865, Bloomingdale's in New York in 1872, and also Wanamaker's in Philadelphia in 1876.

No one retailer or department store can possibly take the credit for producing the first eye-catching staged window display; however, we can certainly look to various individuals who have helped set the standards for today's visual merchandisers.

It was American retail entrepreneur Gordon Selfridge who had grand aspirations to bring the concept of the department store—and with it the language of visual merchandising—to Edwardian London. After leaving his post as managing director of the majestic Marshall Field's department store in Chicago and emigrating to England, he arrived in London with grand designs to build a long-awaited premier, purpose-built, modern department store.

On March 15, 1909, Londoners witnessed the unveiling of Gordon Selfridge's £400,000 (around $700,000) dream. Selfridges became the benchmark of British retailing. Its vast, plate-glass windows were filled with the finest merchandise its proprietor had to offer. Selfridge also revolutionized the world of visual merchandising by leaving the window lights on at night, even when the store was closed, so that the public could still enjoy the presentations while returning home from the theater.

Selfridge also included a few innovations in-store for his customers—including a soda fountain for the sociable and a quiet room for the less so. He was never one to miss out on promotional opportunity. When, in July 1909, Louis Blériot crash-landed his airplane in a field in Kent after flying across the English Channel, Selfridge had the plane packed on a train at 2 a.m. and on display the same morning at 10 a.m. Fifty thousand people queued to see it that day. By 1928, Selfridges had doubled in size to become the

store we now know, due to the hype and success of Gordon Selfridge.

The 1920s saw an explosion of creativity in the arts and fashion, which spilled over into the art of window display, and once again, it was Paris that led the way. Frustrated that their canvases could only be seen in the homes of the rich and famous, many young artists in the city took their skills to the masses. Soon, the arcades of the capital were occupied with Art Deco-inspired themes, and fashion designers now found an innovative and exciting static runway on which to show their creations.

Above
Maybe it is not the most innovative display by today's standards, but Marshall Field's window from the early 1900s caused a public reaction at the time in Chicago.

Below
The coats on the mannequins in this 1950s window display at Printemps in Paris may look elegant, but the mannequins are rigid and not grouped to engage with each other.

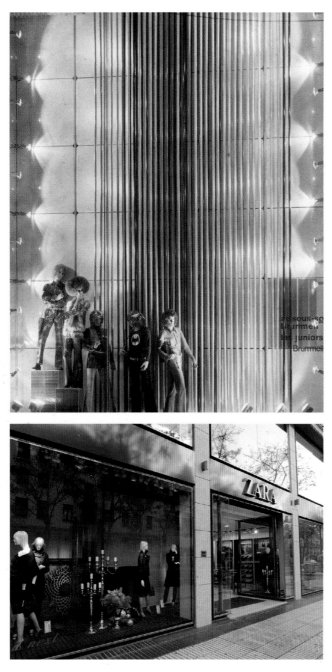

lack of success did not deter other would-be artists from beginning their careers as window dressers. The artist Andy Warhol began his career in the stores of New York while still in college; Jasper Johns, James Rosenquist, and Robert Rauschenberg all worked as window dressers in the 1950s.

It was not only the big department stores that followed the new style of window dressing. As fashion shifted from the couture houses to the major streets and social trends developed, fashion designers worldwide began to make the most of their windows. Pierre Cardin, Mary Quant, and Vivienne Westwood are just a few who told the youth of yesteryear which social tribe they should belong to by dressing their windows to inspire.

Terence Conran was acutely aware of the shifting fashion trends. In 1964, he created a store to match those of the emerging fashion boutiques, but his differed in its type of product: furniture. Chelsea, London, was the epicenter of style and youth culture and Conran was quick to capitalize on it. His first store boasted whitewashed walls, creating a sense of space that came as a revelation to home-owners. Customers who visited his growing empire soon experienced spotlit ceilings, tile floors, and cafés. Nowadays, Habitat still maintains its presence on the British high street, together with other stores such as Liberty and Harvey Nichols that paved the way for the retailers of today; in New York an equivalent is Barneys.

The development of technology in the 1990s and the birth of super-brands like Gucci and Prada saw the evolution of window displays into propaganda machines. With massive marketing budgets behind them, these larger brands were able to produce mass-marketing campaigns that featured the world's most desirable faces and bodies. In the windows of fashion stores, the mannequins that had graciously modeled garments for decades became redundant and were often replaced by huge, glossy photographs of emerging catwalk super-models. Runway shows from the world's fashion capitals were projected on high-tech TV screens, and the clever use of lighting not only enhanced the product but also helped to create ambience and drama.

Thanks to the experiments and experience of the window dressers from yesteryear,

The department stores of New York's Fifth Avenue followed suit. In the 1930s, the surrealist artist Salvador Dalí can be credited with setting the American creative criteria in window display. He was approached to dress two windows for the Bonwit Teller store. Street art took on another dimension when he unveiled his "Narcissus" displays, but it was a step too far: his outrageous pastiches were removed after complaints. Yet Dalí's

Above
By the 1970s, window dressing had begun to reflect the spirit of the age. In this window from Printemps in Paris, the mannequins are displayed in tune with the times, with mirrored plinths suggesting the mirror-balls from the discos of the day.

Below
In the fashion-store chain Zara, stylishly dressed mannequins are complemented by a similarly elegant window scheme, where the message of opulence is suggested simply by the inclusion of candelabras.

today's visual merchandisers have a lot of proven techniques with which to work. Visual merchandisers working in the proliferating fashion-store chains today, for example, are reintroducing the mannequin to the shop window, having acknowledged it to be a successful option for displaying the latest trends in a similar manner from store to store. The Spanish fashion store Zara, for example, employs traditional window-dressing techniques, its innovative window schemes and clever fashion styling placing its windows alongside those of the major luxury brands.

Now that retail brands have not only taken control of the foremost shopping streets in all major cities but have also infiltrated the rural towns and villages, their innovative techniques in visual merchandising have also made an impact on their competitors. In the last decade, brands have pushed the boundaries of visual merchandising not just by creating in-store displays to drive sales and keep the customer inspired but also by introducing new techniques: DJs performing in urban clothing shops; contemporary eateries flanking fashion floors; books and magazines breaking out of their host departments; and fashion shows that can be viewed not only by the fashionistas but also by lunch-time shoppers.

Today, a brand might exist within its own store, but the store can also become a brand in its own right, populating its floor space with other brands, the idea being that together they will generate more sales. This is particularly apparent in the larger department stores like Selfridges, Printemps, and Macy's. Either way, the visual merchandiser's task is to communicate a fundamental message to the public through window displays and in-store visual merchandising.

In the twenty-first century, the latest challenge to the supremacy of the traditional store is the Internet. Shopping from home is not only easier but also price-competitive. Stores are under even more pressure to ensure that their customers return and spend, and it is the visual merchandiser who will be key to attracting and retaining their attention. Fortunately, shopping has always been a social activity, and the thrill of it will always be the major part of the consumer experience. Whether shoppers are out to discover an unexpected bargain, find an item

sought for a long time, or meet up with friends while browsing, it is the job of the retailer to guarantee that they not only purchase but have a positive retail experience. With the help of good visual merchandising, this can easily be achieved.

Above

In the larger department stores, men's fashion collections such as Alexander McQueen, John Galliano, and Dior sit together in one area to create the men's designer room. The design of the floor layout demonstrates carefully considered use of visual merchandising: note its cleverly positioned fixtures, clear signage, and the use of the window at the back of the cash desk, which creates a focal point for customers entering the department.

The Role of
a Visual
Merchandiser

"We are the guys backstage that are stage-managing and producing the whole effect, whereas the buyers are writing the story and providing the content. We are the ones who have to bring it to life."

Alannah Weston, Creative Director, Selfridges

A visual merchandiser's role is to increase sales: first by attracting shoppers into the store through the power of the window display, and then through in-store display and layout, which needs to encourage them to remain in the store, purchase, and have a positive retail experience so that they return.

Individuals wanting to pursue a career in visual merchandising would benefit from being creative, commercial, understanding, and unquestionably hard-working. Long hours, opinionated colleagues and members of the public, and tight deadlines are all common challenges that go with the job. In addition, an awareness not only of fashion trends but also of social, political, and economic trends would be beneficial for any visual merchandiser. No longer do the fashion pages dictate to the retail world; lifestyle trends are as important as apparel. Where individuals take their

holidays and who they listen to on their iPods may well influence the style and direction of where they choose to shop.

Above all, an unbiased outlook is paramount. A successful store may already have its own winning creative formula, and although the visual merchandising manager may be willing to listen to suggestions, he or she will usually want someone with a commercial mind who can help support the existing team. A non-personal view and unopinionated attitude toward the product you may be asked to work with is a necessity. A good visual merchandiser can work with the ugliest and most unsympathetic of products and still come up with great results.

Above
The use of dramatically posed mannequins and simple graphics applied to both the wall and floor create a stunning in-store display at Lane Crawford, Hong Kong.

The day-to-day role of a visual merchandiser

Depending whether visual merchandisers work for a large department store, a multi-store retailer, or an independent boutique, they will be expected to manage and generally oversee the visual presentation of the windows and in-store displays. This will involve liaising with the buying teams to ascertain what has been bought and how best to promote it. As well as laying out complete floors of new season merchandise, they will also be expected to set the overall retail standards for the store. Everyday tasks will include ensuring that the fixtures are replenished with the correct product and that the corresponding signage is present, as well as checking that the windows and in-store displays are still presentable, tidy, and well lit.

Large visual merchandising teams may designate specific roles for individuals to maximize their resources. Individual visual merchandisers working for smaller retailers may be expected not only to dress the windows but to arrange for the outside glass to be cleaned regularly. The responsibilities of visual merchandisers seldom stop at solely dressing mannequins.

Above
The visual merchandiser puts the finishing touches to the grouping before adjusting the lighting, cleaning the window, and inspecting it from outside.

Training

"Visual and merchandising standards are extremely important to us. We educate our staff on an ongoing basis, including seasonal styling seminars and store visits, to ensure there is consistency on a national level. To ensure consistent merchandising standards, we supply visual staff nationally with a 'bible' that outlines the company's visual standards and guidelines for all areas and departments. Visually, we develop extremely detailed directives that are sent out on a monthly basis to all stores. At the end of each season, we conduct a post-mortem exercise across the country for each installation, providing an individual critique."

John Gerhardt, Creative Services Director, Holt Renfrew

Those wishing to enter the profession will usually either take a specific visual merchandising course at a college or university and then seek work experience in-store, or they can apply directly to a store for work experience.

There are several visual merchandising courses available. Students are likely to learn how to place products together, create and install windows, and merchandise shop floors. Many courses will also give an insight into the advantages of the use of color, lighting, and branding. By using many practical exercises together with theory, these two-year courses give a good insight into the world of visual merchandising and provide the student with a useful and recognized qualification.

Short courses are also offered to would-be store owners who prefer a fast-track education and may want to learn specific aspects of visual merchandising.

As in many other careers, work experience can be a valuable asset. And in this industry it is common to rely heavily on work-experience students to fill many positions. As Mark Briggs, creative director from London's Harrods, explains, "Students doing their work placement at Harrods get to cover all aspects of visual merchandising. They get to handle every category of product so that they not only get an understanding of the items but also so they can decide which area they would like to excel in: home, fashion, food, or beauty." Briggs develops experts for every product category in the store; a fashion dresser may not necessarily be confident at grouping kitchenware, for example.

Young, eager students on work experience—depending on the time of the year and the schedule of the visual merchandising team—can find themselves working on a window or sent to clean the stockroom. Either way, their efforts are often recognized, and in a career where visual merchandisers hop from one store to another, positions often become available for those in the right place at the right time. The visual merchandising teams will rely on a full head count to fulfil their hectic programs.

Visual merchandising in a department store

Department stores will give a novice excellent training and knowledge of visual merchandising because of the diverse range of products that they house. The training to be gained from an established team is invaluable.

Traditionally, those entering a visual merchandising team in a department store will begin as dresser or junior visual merchandiser; if they work hard and show that they are willing, they may be promoted within two years to a senior role. Managers are likely to spot potential and develop those they see as future managers by encouraging them to develop their communication and managerial skills, to begin managing a budget and to develop a complete window scheme before they are promoted to a managerial role. Those dressers who enjoy the hands-on practicalities of working on displays may prefer not to pursue a managerial role, given all the administration it involves. A regional department store may have its own visual merchandising team, which takes its lead from the flagship store, but the career path there will be similar to that in the flagship store, with the regional manager controlling the budget and recruitment for the regional store.

Mark Briggs of Harrods recruits most of his 67 staff as students. After completing work experience, they go on to assist him dressing 1.25 miles (2 km) of window space and merchandising 1,000,000 sq ft (92,903 square metres) of shop floor. Mark says that a good structure is key to the smooth running of his team. "Communication is the key word," he explains. "I hold weekly meetings with my team leaders to explain future concepts and promotions to make them feel part of the Harrods family."

Harrods, like many department stores worldwide, employs separate interior and window visual merchandising teams. A visual

merchandiser often has the chance to choose which of the two he or she prefers to excel in; others, however, will be placed according to their merits and talents. Working in both categories will give the trainee visual merchandiser a better overall knowledge and may make the individual more marketable.

Above
Oversized gilt picture frames are used as props in this in-store display to create drama and atmosphere at Lane Crawford, Hong Kong.

Below
Also at Lane Crawford, these immaculately dressed mannequins interact with housewares to make dramatic in-store displays.

A typical department-store visual merchandising structure would be:

Senior Visual Merchandise Manager/Director

Responsibilities

To establish and oversee the creative look of the store.

To liaise with the buying director to ensure that the correct product is promoted.

To work closely with the operation director to guarantee that the store layouts are planned correctly.

To communicate with the marketing director to make certain that the visual merchandising team supports any store product promotions.

To control a payroll and visual merchandising budget.

To purchase relevant props and mannequins.

To recruit qualified staff.

To manage the store's graphics and signage.

Visual Merchandise Manager

Responsibilities

To manage a team.

To liaise with buyers and marketing.

To communicate with the senior visual merchandise manager.

To design and implement in-store and window displays.

To interact with the graphics team.

To liaise with floor managers.

To know competitors.

To communicate with brands.

Senior Visual Merchandiser

Responsibilities

To mentor junior members of the team.

To act as a bridge between visual merchandise manager and floor manager.

To be aware of fashion trends and key looks.

To maintain retail standards.

To communicate with the graphics team.

To educate shop-floor staff.

To work closely with brands to ensure a consistent product representation.

Junior/Dresser Visual Merchandiser

Responsibilities

To maintain retail standards.

To be aware of fashion trends.

To work closely with shop-floor staff to ensure visual guidelines are met.

To understand and be aware of brands.

To present merchandise both creatively and with the maximization of sales in mind.

In addition, a visual merchandising team will include an important support team whose members may include the following:

Carpenters

A carpenter's role within a department store is not just confined to the making of props in the studio; he or she will be instrumental in installing and removing windows and in-store displays. Fully qualified and professionally trained carpenters will also know when a prop needs to be finished to a high standard because it may be placed where the public will scrutinize it up close, and when to compromise on overall quality because it may only be viewed from the front and though glass. Carpenters working in a visual merchandising team will often be able to extend their talents beyond working in wood and will be able to make props from a variety of media.

Painters

Apart from the obvious—painting windows—a painter working in a visual merchandising team may offer a variety of skills. Many are experts in paint effects, and—in conjunction with the carpenters—will be responsible for applying the finishing touches to eye-catching props and window schemes.

Porters

It may seem a luxury to employ porters. However, ensuring that valuable furniture and exquisite props enter and leave the windows in one piece is essential. Most porters will also be responsible for managing and maintaining the stockroom that houses props and mannequins.

Graphic designers

In-house graphics teams are now slowly being disbanded in favor of outside agencies that provide not only the ideas but also the equipment and skill to create a store's artwork. The benefits of an in-house graphics team are, however, unquestionable. Unlike outside contractors, its members will be aware of the store's overall image and, undoubtedly, having them on hand to produce samples that can be edited on-site saves a lot of valuable time. In or out of house, a graphics team is responsible for the consistent application of the store's graphic design to price tags, banners, and promotional information.

Opposite
Paint cans and brushes as props complement brightly colored hosiery to convey this "Colorist" window theme, which would involve the whole visual merchandising team, from managers to graphic designers.

Visual merchandising of chain stores

Chain stores will have a similar visual merchandising structure to that of a department store. However, each store may not have the luxury of its own in-house visual merchandiser. Instead, one visual merchandiser or a team of visual merchandisers may travel from store to store in a chain, covering specific areas of the country. For any major promotions such as Christmas and sales, other visual merchandisers may be drafted in to help. However, visual merchandising is usually undertaken by just one individual. Working for an area manager, the visual merchandiser in a chain will be recruited through the firm's head office and will then follow a career path similar to that of an equivalent role in a department store.

These positions are best suited to organized individuals who enjoy traveling—even traveling abroad as, on many occasions, the stores for which they are responsible are overseas. Of course, those working for a chain whose head office is overseas may also have to travel to that office for briefings.

A visual merchandiser working for a chain of stores will be given guidance and direction from the company's head office. There the visual merchandising manager will design and plan the installation of windows and in-store visual merchandising projects for the entire chain, and will then filter the tasks through to the individual area visual merchandisers. International stores, such as Gap, follow these rules. The Gap head office in the U.S.A., for example, enforces strict guidelines to ensure that the brand is not compromised. It communicates brand strategy and visual guidelines to visual merchandising managers in each of the countries in which Gap has a store, who then delegate tasks to the relevant members of their team.

The flagship store in a chain—usually the largest and most prominent—often has the most elaborate window displays. Because they often vary in size, individual regional stores will have window schemes tailor-made to suit the size of the windows. Budgetary constraints may also mean that they rely on more economical and simpler window schemes, such as printwork that may form a backdrop for the product, which can be installed by just one visual merchandiser.

Communication is paramount for a visual merchandiser in a chain store, as he or she has to ensure that all of the stores launch the same product in their windows at the same time. Promotional activities will also require co-ordination and planning.

The day-to-day role of a chain-store visual merchandiser will include communicating the visual strategy to each of the store managers and store staff, one of whom will be expected to maintain any in-store and window displays. Signage and price tags can be ordered and monitored by the visual merchandiser also.

Above and below
The floor layouts in these Zara stores at Toro and Elx, Spain, were carefully planned, with a display of mannequins and folded products acting as an anchor, or focal point, in the center, while sufficient space was left around it for the customers to circulate.

Visual merchandising of small retail outlets

Smaller independent shops may enlist the help of a self-employed visual merchandiser to help promote their merchandise. "Freelancers," as they are often called, can change the look and atmosphere of a store in a matter of hours. Because they generally work on a project-fee basis, freelancers are usually fast and efficient. Most of these creative individuals have trained within an established and renowned visual team and have contacts who can manufacture props and signage for them. A freelancer may specialize in designing windows or in in-store visual merchandising, or may offer both services. Some may also specialize in fashion styling, while others may excel at product grouping. It is always best to ask to see freelancers' portfolios before engaging them, as these will contain examples of their work.

Most freelancers find their work by word of mouth; a stunning window acts as a good marketing tool not only for the store but also for its creator. Clearly the more skilled and efficient freelancers are, the more work they may acquire.

On some occasions an independent store owner will spot the creative potential in a member of staff and encourage him or her to dress the windows and arrange the in-store displays. With no formal training, this can be risky: not only will the makeshift visual merchandiser have no mentor to learn from, he or she may also pick up bad habits that will not transfer well into a reputable visual merchandising team in the future. In the smaller retail outlet, arranging for a member of staff to attend a short course in visual merchandising would be beneficial.

Above
In Trust Nobody, Barcelona, simple brackets are used to support shoes at eye level with neatly folded items placed directly below. The simplicity of the fixtures make them easy for shopping as well as replenishing.

Measuring success

It is not always easy to gauge the success of a window display or how effective an in-store display is. Despite the hard work that visual merchandisers may put in, retailers can be competitive within their own stores. A well-presented window may create overwhelming sales, for which the buyers may take the credit, attributing the success to the products they selected. However, a window that performs badly will undoubtedly be blamed on the visual merchandiser.

In the overall scheme, it is important for retailers to realize that changing the window display may not generate sudden sales, and that the long-term effect of how the brand is evolving through the use of consistently good windows and in-store displays is more important. Quick wins can often be achieved; however, a structured, achievable plan— which may include advance preparation and

allocation of personnel set against the budget—is more realistic in ensuring that sales and the reputation and image of the store grow as a result of the visual merchandising. Forming a professional relationship with the buyers and shop-floor staff will undoubtedly help visual merchandisers prove their worth and expertise. Together they should be able to share the success of the store's visual merchandising.

Above
In Colette, Paris, simple but effective bust forms are dressed to inspire and inform the customers of the latest seasonal trends. The collections are strategically placed close by.

Store Design

What is store design?

Various department stores worldwide have been molded into amazing show-stopping retail emporia. With their grand façades, Harrods in London—whose thousands of light bulbs glow like a shopper's paradise—and Samaritaine, Paris' largest department store, have always stood the test of time. With the invention of visual merchandising during the 1980s, however, retailers saw the **necessity to offer the customers the same experience in-store. Store design became crucial to success. Today, many designer outlets in particular spend as much time and investment on their store's design as on their collections.**

Store design unites all aspects of visual merchandising: window display and interior design as well as fixtures and lighting. Visual merchandisers, architects, and interior designers have always worked hand in hand to create retail environments that are inspirational yet commercial and above all, a canvas on which visual merchandisers can demonstrate their skills. It would be sense-less for an architect to develop a store's interior without first understanding the visual merchandiser's needs and requirements. A good store design will show products to their best advantage. Walkways, lighting, and signage are all major features that need to be discussed even before the important fixtures are designed. Some retailers may also enlist the help of interior decorators, lighting designers, and artists to help create the in-store ambience.

Above
The architects of the Prada store in New York, Rem Koolhaas's Office for Metropolitan Architecture, did not just stop at providing a backdrop for the merchandise; they also created a retail space that can be converted into a performance space at the touch of a button. The ramp that opens up to reveal a stage for performances is situated opposite a fixed seating area, creating a sense of theater and providing an ambience to attract customers to the store.

Below
Great care and attention have clearly been given to the lighting in this store for Alexander McQueen in Milan, designed by William Russell. Lighting is completely concealed in the ceiling and along the perimeter walls, with all plugs, light bulbs, and unsightly grills hidden. A pillar with a surrounding seat anchors the whole space and is used as a centerpiece for movement around the floor, while muted light colors provide an easy backdrop for any fashion collection.

Why is store design important?

The design of a store can help support the brand image as well as underpin a successful retail strategy. Retailers rely on the design of the store to entice customers inside. While some retailers prefer a more subtle store design, others like to shock and inspire, creating stores that generate hype and discussion.

Before choosing which road to go down, a retailer should first consider the demographics of its customers. Traditional shoppers would possibly not be impressed if their local department store turned futuristic and contemporary. Most retail chains have a proven set format that they use when opening stores. Established retailers such as Britain's Marks & Spencer would perhaps suffer if they unexpectedly designed an avant-garde store; the risk would be too high and might unnerve their loyal following. There are times, however, when it may be advantageous to break the mold. In September 2003, for example, Selfridges embraced a more contemporary outlook and departed from the turn-of-the-twentieth-century style of its Oxford Street building in London when it opened a futuristic-style store in Birmingham, England. The building was part of the rejuvenation of the city's 1960s Bullring shopping center. With hundreds of silver disks adorning the blue organic shell, the new store is either loathed or loved by the locals, but, as Gordon Selfridge would have appreciated, at least it is noticed and opinions are formed.

Above

Future Systems' design for the Birmingham Selfridges, which opened in 2003, has become an iconic part of the city's architecture. Like the flagship store on London's Oxford Street, it does not have its name emblazoned across the entrance.

Gordon Selfridge himself said that the store didn't need a name—everyone would know the building by its very design—and the new store in Birmingham follows the precedent in spectacular style.

Who designs the store?

must have foreseen that his opulent yet quirky creation would create waves among their existing loyal customers. To enforce his design, Starck also created an exclusive collection of crystal for sale in the store.

Before starting on the store design, the more information the architect is given about the product and the brand, the easier it will be to understand the task. An architect needs to be aware of the product items to be sold and the stock densities for each fixture, because fixtures need to be functional as well as part of an overall design concept. Product adjacencies are also key in creating a cohesive floor, and of course the all-important cash desks, stockrooms, and offices need to be incorporated into the final design, all of which are part of the remit of the visual merchandiser (see Chapter Five).

An architect will start by preparing concept ideas for the client to approve; the initial ideas will seldom be what may have been expected. Once the designs have been approved, the architect will produce floor plans and a timeline of how the overall building work will be completed, as well as the ever-important budget. The architect will also suggest building contractors and specialists to build the shop fit and will manage and oversee the whole process. Contractors will include builders, electricians, painters, and carpenters. Between them lies the responsibility to ensure that the deadline for the store opening is met.

At some time all retailers will have to consult with an architect, either to design a new store, renovate an existing one, or rejuvenate an area of their shop. Normally, they will consult an architect experienced in commercial practice, which differs from domestic architecture due to the need to take public access into consideration. On most occasions, retailers will choose architects with experience in store design because of their knowledge and proven track record. Others, however, may challenge young talented designers to create their stores.

In designing stores, many architects will add their signature style, which more often than not is why they were commissioned in the first place. When the famous French crystal manufacturer Baccarat approached the noted designer and architect Philippe Starck to design its headquarters in Paris, the directors

Above
In this clever use of space in crowded Tokyo, Klein Dytham has created a covered catwalk suspended above the street for Undercover Lab.

Below
Here Philippe Starck has created a juxtaposition of free-standing modern cabinets set against the backdrop of a traditional-style fresco, which is sympathetic to the style of Baccarat collection.

Opposite
Water and electricity don't usually mix, yet here in Maison Baccarat's store in Paris, Starck has suspended a lit chandelier in a contemporary aquarium, creating a quirky yet stunning visual.

How does store design work?

The main purpose of store design is to show a product to its best advantage. This is achieved through a combination of ambience, functionality, and an inviting design. Each store will be different, depending on its product; a supermarket will be more concerned with functionality, while a retailer of luxury goods will want to create the right ambience.

Independent store owners can certainly take the risk of promoting more adventurous store design. Some of the most imaginative designs can be found in Japan. The streets of Tokyo hide many interesting retail outlets, the most exciting of which are hidden in the backstreets instead of taking center stage on the main shopping thoroughfares. The four small overcrowded islands, thousand of miles from the West, are a melting pot of creativity. Small spaces are transformed into retail galleries. The Sony Centre in the Ginza region of Tokyo is an interactive techno-shopper's emporium: floors of the latest gadgets and software are available to the customers to sample, plasma screens cover ceilings, and interactive information demonstrates their innovative ideas.

A Bathing Ape in Japan primarily sells casual clothes and fashion accessories displayed in Perspex racks mounted on a glass floor which offers a view of the basement. The brand has achieved cult status not only in Japan but also worldwide because of its quirky product and store design.

Offering a complete contrast in terms of space, Habitat opened its flagship store on London's Regent Street in 2006 in the shell of what was once an old movie theater (as well as a church and meat market), where Queen Victoria watched her first film. Tom Dixon, Habitat's creative director, introduced contemporary fixtures that sit within the original neo-Egyptian architecture. The marriage of old and new design makes the store an inviting prospect, with its fascinating insight into London's Victorian past.

Milan's Corsa Como has attracted the world's fashion pack for years. It is hidden away at the end of an unassuming walkway, but the customer's first impression on entering the store is the vast scale of the space. An alfresco dining area fills the courtyard and then branches onto the retail area and a restaurant. Stairs lead to a bookshop and finally to an exhibition space on the second floor. The fixtures are not the most costly or innovative—most of them were at some stage retro pieces of furniture or lighting—but positioned together, they create a unique selling environment. Not all store designs need vast budgets; resourceful and interesting schemes often make the most exciting shops.

Above left
The impressive Prada store by Herzog and de Meuron in Tokyo, Japan, has become an iconic piece of architecture because of its incredible design. The skeletal form on the outside gives the customers a view of the inside from the pavement.

Above right
The use of an eclectic mix of furniture, including design classics, and a busy floor layout gives the impression of a sophisticated and edgy market, making Corso Como in Milan accessible yet interesting to the shopper.

Opposite
In Habitat's store on Regent Street, London, the original architecture of this former movie theater has been used to good effect. It has created a contemporary retail space within a very traditional backdrop, resulting in an eye-catching and inviting store.

Store study:
Kurt Geiger

Rebecca Farrar-Hockley is the buying and creative director for luxury shoe brand Kurt Geiger. Not only does Kurt Geiger have several independent U.K. stores, the company also has prominent concessions in Harrods, Selfridges, and other major department stores, including La Rinascente in Milan. The new flagship store in London's Regent Street is the company's largest and most prestigious to date. The architects appointed to design the store were Found Associates, with whom Kurt Geiger has collaborated successfully in the past.

Rebecca Farrar-Hockley and the chief executive officer of Found Associates, Richard Found, discuss the key issues of designing a store and their expectations for the visual merchandising.

On the subject of designing a store with visual merchandising in mind for Kurt Geiger

Rebecca Farrar-Hockley "Shoe shops present an enormous challenge for designers and visual merchandisers because the whole presentation is about display. Customers do not shop the same way for shoes as they do for clothes because they cannot help themselves to the product and simply take it straight to the cash desk; you cannot have every size available on the shelf, and often the product is too expensive to leave unattended. In effect, the whole shop is like a large window display. Clearly the correct visual presentation can affect the overall sales; there should be no room for human error. It is important that Kurt Geiger shops are designed in a way that means they need little dressing. Because of the number of stores we have, it can be hard to maintain them effectively. An easy, fool-proof store design suits us best."

On the collaboration between retailer and designer

Richard Found "We always ask the client for a detailed written brief, because it will force them to think about requirements and needs. It then helps us to bring more sustenance in providing the answers."

RFH "It is so important that both parties have a strong professional relationship. With all our projects, Richard has understood the complications of our shoe business and is fully aware of the brand image we want to promote."

On increasing customer count

RF "Focal points are extremely important to store design. For the Kurt Geiger store in Liverpool, [which] has no window because the

Above and opposite
Using a specially designed in-store display will let passersby know about the product available inside a store that has no window. Here, this mirrored display in the Liverpool store is both attractive and practical, carrying a wide range of luxury shoes.

store is positioned in a mall, we designed a glass shelf fixture that is placed at the front of the store and houses many shoes. It attracts attention and draws customers in."

RFH "We call it the miracle fixture, because it works. It allows us to have a window that looks great yet needs no maintenance. The unit can be dressed with key colored shoes and still create impact."

RF "It becomes a kaleidoscope. When customers pass, it changes perspective and creates movement."

On stock densities

RF "It is important to understand just how much product the store is required to show. It would be pointless designing a store that is beautiful yet impractical."

RFH "Future growth is also important and needs to be taken into consideration. I have to make sales grow and make sure I have a good turnover. In the future, I might need to introduce more products that will eat into the valuable sales floor."

On fixture requirements

RF "Three or four tried-and-tested fixture configurations are the main proven require-ments that will produce good results. There would be no point [in] altering the shelf heights that work so well in other stores, for example."

RFH "When working for another retailer, I once merchandised a department that had been designed with many extra fixture components, supposedly made to support the visual merchandising. I found, however, that the fixtures were sufficient by themselves because the product was visually very strong, and so the extra components were not needed. Good fixtures blend into the

Above
Simple fixtures and a neutral white background provide a versatile and practical backdrop for the shoes and the overall floor layout is specific to this product. With only one shoe from each pair on display, and usually only one shoe of each size, the stockroom, which generally takes up to 40 per cent of the retail space in a shoe store, is sited conveniently near the cash desk at the rear.

background, allowing the products to stand out."

On the use of color

RF "A relatively blank canvas for the products to sit within will give you stronger flexible options. Strong colored walls may clash with colorful shoes."

RFH "A men's area may, however, require the use of color, because of the nature of men's shoes: they mostly come in brown or black. A strong, colorful background can help show them to their full advantage."

On lighting

RF "All aspects of design are crucial. If you fail in one thing, you can fail at everything. Lighting is one of the most fundamental aspects of design. Bad lighting can change the appearance of the product; a yellow light on brown leather can turn the shoe red. Lighting that omits a white light will give a more accurate overall effect."

On brand identity

RFH "I prefer to have a thread that becomes a common element that is synonymous with Kurt Geiger, rather than an identical format for every shop."

RF "The size and position of the store may also dictate what you can achieve with the design concept. The Regent Street shop, unlike the Liverpool store, is part of a historic run of listed buildings. The design process includes many legal implications and building requirements."

Above
This artist's impression shows the Regent Street store that houses women's shoes on the first floor and men's in the basement. A section of the first floor has been removed so that the customers outside on the sidewalk can have a preview of the men's collection downstairs.

Windows

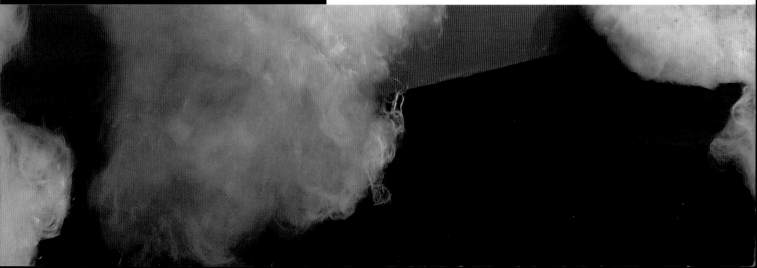

"If Selfridges were a magazine,
the windows would be the front cover."

Alannah Weston, Creative Director, Selfridges

There is no doubt that windows can be used to sell if they are eye-catching and innovative. They are the only major marketing tool that you do not have to pay for because they are part of the store's architecture, apart from the initial set-up costs, so it is worth making the most of them. Many retailers still spend a vast amount of their marketing budget creating works of art; others present their products simply, yet effectively. Some, however, never use their windows to their full capacity. Whether a window is large—similar to that of a department store—or simply a modest-sized one looking into a store, each needs to be

carefully planned. A well-dressed window display not only attracts shoppers into the store, it also enforces the retailer's brand image. It can act as an advertising tool and also give an insight into what is available in-store.

Depending on the type of store, different factors will drive the make-up of the window display at different times, and consequently the amount of creative licence allowed to the visual merchandiser. A large department store (or even a small retail outlet) may wish to attract attention to its store by creating a display with a noteworthy theme intended to cause a reaction. This type of window is less likely to be driven by product alone, and so is steered instead by the marketing or buying department anxious to promote a particular product or trend into which they have bought heavily or wanting to front an advertising campaign. A product-driven window can be used equally in a department store or small retail outlet, but it is more likely to be the main type of window in a chain store, where the need to reach the mass market is particularly vital.

Whatever the driving force behind the window display, there are a number of considerations to be taken into account when planning the window, including the type of window, the best way to group products, whether or not to introduce a theme or scheme, and the use of props, lighting, graphics, and signage.

Above
Selfridges' "Future Punk" window scheme features a contemporary view of the punk era. Neon lighting and brightly colored mannequins were the main theme running throughout the London store.

Opposite
These windows consist of simple lines and bold colorful "Shapes" to promote a revival of the 1960s fashion look.

Getting to know your windows

Before attempting to design and dress a window, it is best to understand the space and depth of the window you might be expected to work with, as well as its practical features which will affect what you can put into the window and how.

Window size and style

The scale of the window you have to work with may affect what you can achieve. There is no standard size or shape of window in major shopping streets; every store window will differ. Larger windows will require a lot more merchandise and more props to fill them; others may require less. In addition to the scale of the window, there are a variety of styles, the most common of which include closed or open-back windows and shadow boxes. Thought also needs to be given to shops with no window at all.

Closed windows

These are usually seen in department stores. With a large pane of glass at the front (facing the audience in the street), a solid back wall and two solid side walls and a door, these windows resemble a room. They are the most thrilling to dress because you can capture the public's attention from just one angle: the street.

Closed windows need considerable planning before they are dressed. Usually large, they will require a lot of merchandise to fill them. Props will also have to be big, and possibly made in multiples, thus adding to the cost. However, expensive merchandise can be used, providing that the door is secure and customers will not be able to gain access and tamper with the presentation. From a design point of view, because they are seen from only one angle, the dressing needs only to be front-facing.

Open-back windows

These have no back wall but may have side walls. Many retailers prefer them because they make the interior of the shop visible from the outside. This does however mean that the interior will need to be maintained and look attractive at all times. These windows can be more difficult to dress because they are viewed from both outside and inside. Unlike in the closed window, expensive merchandise would not be secure, so it is not suitable for use in this type of window. Thought also needs to be given to the possibility that customers may also be able to touch the display.

No window

Shopping arcades often have good examples of stores with no windows. The whole front of the store is exposed to the public with only a grill to separate the store from the public in the evening. Because there is no door or partition stopping customers from entering, these stores encourage the public to walk inside and browse. There may seem to be no window-display requirement; however, display bases can be positioned just inside the entrance with presentations dressed to attract the customers.

Above
A closed window can be treated like a stage, as shown in this Zara store, in Stockholm, where the window scheme faces the audience: the passing shopper in the street.

Below
Like a closed window, open-back windows should be dressed toward the customer in the street, but because they give a view into the store, both the window and the store sides need to be well maintained. This example shows Stella McCartney, New York.

Corner windows

Here, the windows wrap around a corner. In these windows groupings should be dressed toward the center of the arc. Clever use of groupings can help lead the customer from one side of the window all the way around to the other and on toward the entrance of the store.

Arcade windows

Here, the door is set back from the windows. In this case, part of the display should be facing the sidewalk to gain the customer's attention, and another part of it should be set for display on the return, leading the customer toward the door.

Shadow boxes

Stores that specialize in small items such as jewelry often rely on shadow boxes to attract the customer's attention. These miniature windows are placed at eye level to allow close scrutiny of the merchandise.

Angled windows

These are angled back to the entry. This type of window is gradually being replaced on major shopping streets, but if you are faced with such a window, remember that groupings and products should be displayed parallel to the pane of glass—not to the sidewalk. This is because customers are more likely to stop and stand in front of the pane of glass on their way to the door. Dressing a window like this also gives you the advantage of being able to work with the whole surface area of the glass.

Above left
The entrance to a store with arcade windows is further away from the street, so the role of window dressing here is to draw the customer along the window and into the store, as is the case with Max Studio, Los Angeles.

Above right
A corner window will attract attention from two angles. It is therefore a key window, so it is important to ensure that it is always eye-catching—as does Harvey Nichols in London.

Below
Positioned at eye-level, the shadow box is the perfect tool in which to present smaller, more precious items, as demonstrated at Cartier in Selfridges, London.

CALVIN KLE

Window set-up

Before designing a window, the visual merchandiser needs to understand what is available to work with. Ideally, an experienced visual merchandiser would like a blank canvas to work on that has certain features.

Solid wooden walls

A closed window will always benefit from having strong, solid walls. The back wall forms a backdrop to the window display. Together with the side walls, it should have an even surface that can be painted or covered to co-ordinate with the window scheme. All the walls should also be strong enough to take nails or screws.

Floor panels

MDF removable floor panels are easy to take out and cover, either with fabrics or PVC. They can also hold nails and screws. Being able to alter the flooring in a window can dramatically change the whole appearance of the presentation. Some smaller retailers prefer a fixed floor that is painted every time the scheme changes, while others may prefer a solid, fixed wooden or stone floor that is not altered each time the window is dressed. Both are acceptable but need to be taken into consideration when planning the window scheme. A solid stone floor will not be suitable for setting up a

mannequin because it may not be possible to hammer a nail into such a dense surface (see page 193).

Ceiling grid

A sturdy metal grid painted the same color as the ceiling so that it blends in is of the utmost importance in any window; you may want to hang banners, props, or even mannequins from it at some point. In the longer term, it will mean that holes don't have to be made in the walls for screws and bolts, necessitating repair work before the next dressing.

Secure door

In a closed window, a concealed door will not only enable you to enter and exit the window, it will also secure any expensive products. Ideally a door in a closed window is best positioned in a side wall—not in the back wall where it would dominate the window display and would be in full view of the customers. A good-quality locking device is also recommended.

If you are working on a particularly tall window, mannequins can be elevated on plinths to help fill the larger space.

Above
In this Printemps window in Paris, featuring Calvin Klein merchandise, the locked door is discreetly positioned in the back right-hand corner. Painted the same color as the walls and with no visible handle, it is as inconspicuous as possible.

Lighting tracks

Many of the greatest windows are made even more eye-catching by the clever use of lighting. This is only possible if the window is equipped with high-quality lighting fixtures. We will explore lighting requirements later in the book (see page 90).

Electric sockets

It is advantageous to have a few sockets in any window. They should be hidden either side of the window next to the glass. Like the door, customers should not be able to spot them on the back wall. It is also wise to install a couple in the ceiling close to the glass and out of sight.

Window shade

Many visual merchandisers prefer to create their masterpieces while hidden from the public. A window shade also hides the mess caused while either dressing or stripping a window.

Easy access

Moving larger props or furniture items into a window will be effortless if the door is wide enough. The visual merchandiser also needs access to be able to maneuver the items through the department at the back of the window.

Speakers

In many department or large stores, security is paramount. While a visual merchandiser may be locked away dressing a window it is important that he or she keeps in contact with the outside world via in-store announcements.

Fire sprinklers

Fires have been known to start in a window because of faulty wiring or an overheated light fixture. A fully operational sprinkler system will help prevent such fires.

Above
Painted the same color as the ceiling, the lighting grid can be used to hold the lighting tracks, and also props and products, a technique seen here.

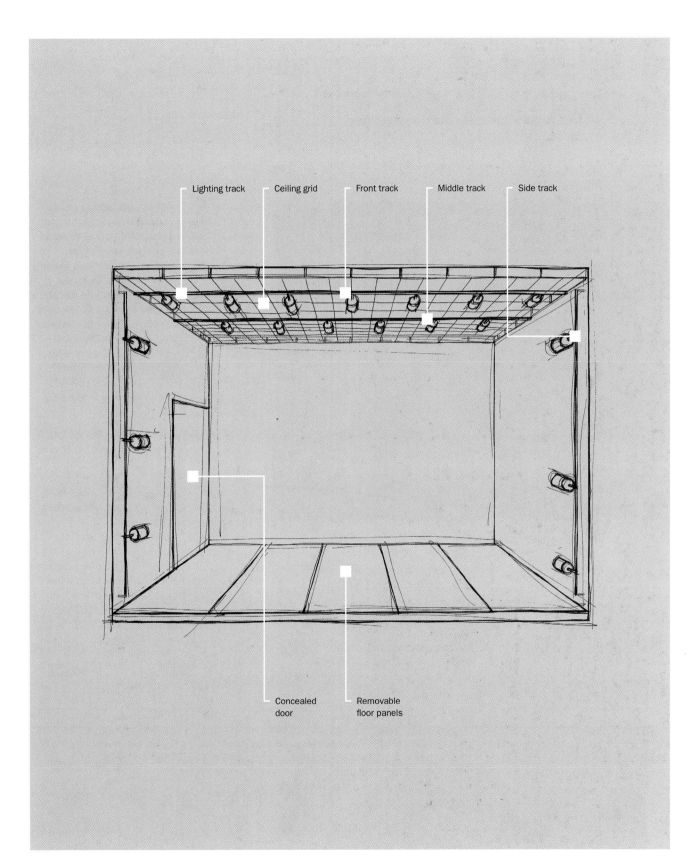

Lighting track   Ceiling grid   Front track   Middle track   Side track

Concealed
door

Removable
floor panels

Planning a window display

Once you are familiar with your canvas—your window—you can then start to plan your display. At this point you also need to consider what you are aiming to achieve with your display. Are you aiming to shock, attract, or cause a buzz, as large department stores such as Barneys in New York or Harvey Nichols in London have done? There are numerous reasons why a visual merchandiser will choose to design a window in a particular way, but first and foremost he or she must ensure that the window theme reflects or is sympathetic to the products being sold in-store.

Window displays will often take the form of a story, incorporating other elements or props (see pages 62–7) that either have something in common with the merchandise or may be completely unrelated but still maintain an artistic balance between props and product. Some retailers like to treat their customers with windows that show no merchandise, yet sell the image of the store or an event occurring in-store; pieces of art, live performances, and animated sets have been used successfully in this way. During sale times it is not uncommon to use merchandise alone to create a window display. With all of these factors in mind, the visual merchandiser will then consider which option is best for a particular project.

"The first step when designing a window is to define a theme and the spirit in which you want to put things forward. Then, you have to find THE idea: that very special idea which will make the difference visually."

Franck Banchet, Creative Director, Printemps

Above
In this "politically correct" window composed of graphics and a mannequin, Topshop in London ensures that its customers understand that it does not sell real fur. It gets its message across by using cuddly toys to create a fur coat.

Above
Windows need not always be used to promote any specific product. They can be designed to stop passing potential customers in their tracks, as in this window in Printemps, Paris, where dancers perform live in the window.

Below
A large graphic dominates the window, also at Printemps, compensating for the size of the actual product on display; lipsticks displayed in front of it are not out of place. Through careful balance, the size of the woman's face is counterbalanced by the large plinth.

Creating a window display that will have an emotional yet thought-provoking effect on the customers is not always easy. Alannah Weston from Selfridges, London, believes that the execution and the language of a display are vital. "Brilliant execution is at the heart of good window display," she says. "Not having too many ideas, having a great composition and really being able to tell a story are so important when designing a window display. Here at Selfridges we are lucky enough to have so many windows that we are able to create a narrative running through them, whether that is very literal or whether it's abstract. It's also about developing a language to speak within the windows. The language could be a series of colors, shapes, or textures. You do not have much time to grab the attention of the public; you need to grab them right as they are passing, but at the same time there should be details that want to make the customers stay there longer if they want to. And of course, the windows need to be informative."

Alannah is also keen to enlist the help of artists and other noted creative individuals to design her windows. "One of our creative strategies is to collaborate with others, whether that means working with a fashion designer to create an exclusive window or bring in either unknown or famous artists to design a complete scheme," she adds. "I find they all bring such huge talent to the store. We understand how to work with them and also how to get the best from them. It's good to have an open mind and ask for other points of view."

Above
In its "Future Punk" windows, which on the one hand might be slightly disturbing to some viewers, Selfridges in London provocatively cross-fertilizes the subjects of sex and kitchenware.

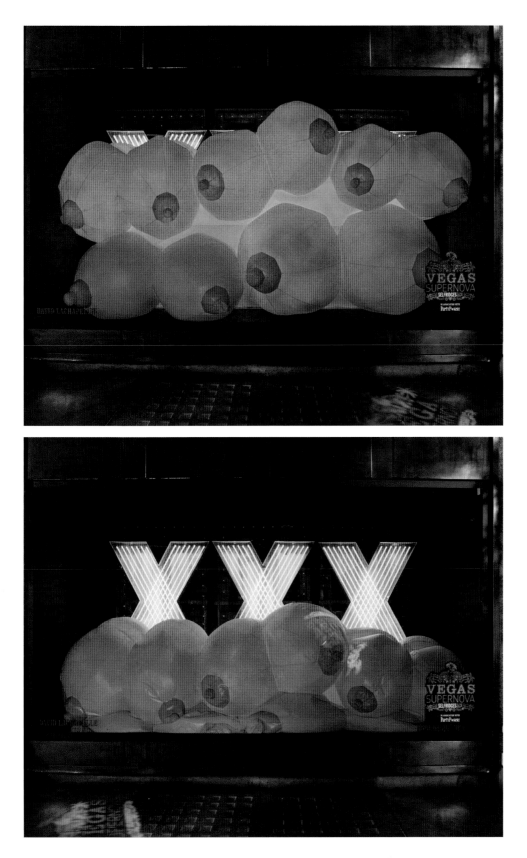

Above
Designed by David LaChapelle, inflatable breasts fill a Selfridges window in London to promote the theme of the seedier side of Las Vegas for a month-long "Vegas Supernova" promotion, the aim of which was to offer an experience other than shopping and to attract a different kind of customer to the store. The dynamism of the display was heightened by the fact that as the breasts deflated, neon signs hidden behind were slowly revealed.

Themes and schemes

Both "themes" and "schemes" are familiar words to a visual merchandiser. They refer to the creative element that will be used to support the product. They are both related, giving the window or windows a thread that will pull the overall look together. A theme or scheme should be well planned and thought through. Visual merchandisers use them to create drama, to tell a story, and to inspire. They can be seasonal or a commentary upon social, political, or economic trends.

A theme is the main topic of the window presentation. It should include the color, the props, and the relevant merchandise that will make the overall idea come to life. A swimwear theme may include sand, palm trees, and a blue wall, thus giving the feel of a beach. Even a store with one window should have a window theme.

Schemes suit stores with many windows, like department stores such as Macy's or Selfridges, London. A scheme takes on the theme but may be adapted so that each window is different, yet tells the same message. A beach window may have

another positioned next to it with a yacht and a blue floor; the next may have a hotel balcony as its main feature. It is important that the scheme is cohesive and consistent.

In many instances window themes and schemes will be carried into the store and used in the in-store displays as well. When used properly, such displays will project a stronger message to the customer. Printwork such as graphics or signage reflecting the window message is the most effective and economical way of carrying the themes in-store. A theme or scheme can also be replicated in the form of in-store displays at designated areas within the store to carry the window theme inside. It is always worth considering where to place in-store displays to gain maximum exposure; extra mannequins or props can incur additional costs.

Above
The best way of viewing a window scheme is from across the street. Here at Harvey Nichols, London, large graphics, mannequins and props are used to create impact.

Above
Harvey Nichols, in its true
outlandish style, makes the most
of its tall windows by using every
available space to create an
innovative window scheme.

MANDARINA DUCK

Chain stores often invest time and money presenting their flagship store in an eye-catching way. Clearly because the flagship store is larger, the window scheme can be dramatic and create more impact. The challenge for the visual merchandising manager for a chain is to deliver the same message through the smaller stores as well. This can be done by using a common thread, such as a color, a graphic, or a prop. All the windows are likely to be different sizes, even within chains, so often more than one option of display needs to be designed and produced.

Deciding on a window theme is not always easy. There may be a number of factors hindering creative license. The budget immediately springs to mind, but more important may be the need to design around specific items of merchandise selected by the retailer. On many occasions, especially with stores on major shopping streets, the

merchandise you can use may have already been targeted for the windows, possibly due to its presence in a major advertising campaign. This will generally be the same for certain sale items that need to be cleared quickly from the store. In that case, it is always best to start off with a simple yet effective design that will win the support of the retailer.

Understanding the products and the perceived image of the store will always be an advantage. More often than not, a store owner enlisting the help of a professional visual merchandiser will expect the product to be presented well and to be the prominent feature within the window, with props used in a supporting role. If, however, you have more creative freedom to choose the product, then you should first understand the theme and then consider what look and message you hope to project to the customers. For

Above
Window and in-store displays can be based around a permanent theme. Product designer Marcel Wanders extends his futuristic yellow mannequins in-store from the branding for this Mandarina Duck travel store in London, upscaling the figure to create a spectacular oversized giant, inspired by Jonathan Swift's *Gulliver's Travels*, which links the two floors. Yellow is also used as an accent on both mannequins and props within the store.

When looking for an idea for a story or theme for your window, try to be imaginative and inspirational. Remember that trying to recreate a realistic setting will look forced and unnatural if the mannequin is not suited to a particular pose, such as holding a champagne glass or a dancing stance.

example, choosing a selection of traditional furniture and home accessories to go with a contemporary window theme may not work, as it will create a less direct statement. It is always wise to research the product and the window scheme beforehand. Fashion dressers should also look for key trends that can inspire the public. A 1960s fashion revival collection may sit better with furniture from the same era against a black-and-white drop than among an ethnic or rural setting. The product on most occasions will help dictate what the overall window presentation will look like. It is best to start by brainstorming and ascertain what message you expect the customer to perceive from the presentation; rarely is the first idea put into action. One should also consider the style and shape of the products and what would support them.

Above
Part of a range of windows from Topman, these windows show how a theme can be carried from the flagship store through to the smallest of outlets in the chain. In the window of the flagship store in London, a shed covered in red-and-white gingham dominates the window. Rather than taking the shed as a theme through to the smaller stores, gingham is chosen and adapted for use in another store with a back to its window.

Color

The use of color offers an economical and a dramatic effect that can easily be changed to suit a window theme. There is no room for subtlety when choosing a color for a window display. Strong, bold colors will make a difference, whereas an off-white instead of a pure white may not be noticeable from outside. Stripes, checks, and fabric applications will help create theater (see pages 78–83). By simply taking a color from an individual piece of merchandise and replicating it on the wall of the window with paint, you will already have created a co-ordinated theme.

Sex, politics, and social statements

These have often been used as window themes. Shocking a customer will undoubtedly get a reaction and, therefore, the attention of that customer, although sometimes not quite the reaction the retailer expects. Live models and pole dancers have all been featured in Selfridges' windows. Alannah Weston insists that the theme is paramount in creating a successful window: "The theme is important because it tells the customer where you are in terms of what's going on in the world…A lot of our themes might come from the major fashion shows or even the art world, or they may come from what's going on culturally. That gives us a very strong direction, and then you build your language on top of that. My team are incredible because they come from different backgrounds: some are from art backgrounds, some from fashion—I even have someone who studied construction. They all have great ideas, and that is what makes our windows so contemporary."

Metallic colors have a festive feel, but will also attract viewers at night during longer winter nights as they will reflect surrounding streetlights and other lights.

Above
The use of a bold, dynamic blue on the back walls and on the mannequins provides a dramatic backdrop to these "Afro Chic" windows.

Above

Selfridges' "Vegas Supernova" window scheme in London, here featuring neon pole dancers, was inspired by the city's centenary and the Vegas-like glitz concurrently circulating in the fashion world. By adopting such a theme, Selfridges was able to create a window scheme that caused a buzz among the public.

Christmas

For many retailers, Christmas is the time
when the visual merchandising team excels
with its window schemes and themes. Stores
in most major cities compete for the best
windows. Large budgets and huge amounts
of time are spent preparing these festive
extravaganzas. The months of November
and December are prime selling times for
retailers, and not to enter the competition
would be short-sighted and naive.

Above
Specially commissioned, full-scale
topiary trees are the main feature of
this elaborate Christmas presentation.

Below
Although the theme of this Christmas
window from Harvey Nichols in London
may be a socially aware one—that
of recycling—but clever planning and
creativity still produce a festive display.

Budgeting

Retailers will expect big promotions to draw more attention than usual to the store. These will be costly, and it is essential to plan and budget for such events. An annual window budget should be divided to cover all the costs of the planned window schemes. Most retailers will mix expensive and overstated windows with more modestly priced schemes during the course of a year.

A Christmas scheme will always incur the most cost. Any seasonal window will need to be planned early; many prop-makers, freelance dressers, and window technicians are in demand. It is always wise to ensure that any extra help required is budgeted for and booked in advance.

Multiples of the same objects are a quick solution for a more economical window scheme.

Above
A theme as simple as various shades of blue paper clipped to wires and suspended from the ceiling grid creates an interesting yet economical backdrop for a fashion presentation in this Topshop window, London.

Props

Once you have chosen your theme and scheme and your merchandise, it is then time to consider the props you will need before thinking about the layout of the window itself. Props, as the name suggests, are objects that visually support the items for sale. A window display can include one prop or a collection. A prop can have empathy with the products, or cleverly have nothing in common with the merchandise at all. A padded silk box would be a conventional way to support a diamond ring; a roll of barbed wire would be a contemporary way of showing the same piece. One stand-alone prop can be as effective as a whole window scheme fashioned from many. Props enhance a window or an interior display, and they work in the same way on film sets or a theatrical stage. They can be purchased or custom-made. Other merchandise items can also be use as a prop, such as a stock item of furniture used as a backdrop for a fashion scheme. Such props are both economical and commercial because one would not need to pay for them to be made; they can display a price tag and can be sold themselves.

The general rule for props is that they should not overpower yet still support the product: a basic mix of two-thirds props to one-third merchandise is usually best. This may seem an odd balance, but the props are there to support the theme and to provide drama, so they need to be bold enough to create an impression. Too much merchandise can interfere with the artistic composition—unless that is the intention, such as during a clearance sale, when the aim is to focus on the reduction message. Skilled visual merchandisers, however, will have the confidence to ignore this rule if preferable. There should always be interaction between the props and the product. A potted plant placed at the foot of a mannequin will only draw attention for the wrong reasons because it will undoubtedly look out of place and have no relevance to the merchandise it is supporting. It is best to avoid props that are personal favorites if they have nothing in common with the window theme. Small boutiques with no visual guidance are often the worst offenders in this common habit; old pieces of furniture, drapes and artificial flowers unthoughtfully placed in a window with no relevance to the merchandise will look dull and out of place.

Many newcomers to the world of visual merchandising may be concerned about the cost of such items. Of course, a well-made prop may put the retailer on the same ladder as the major department stores. Some of the best windows, however, are crafted not with a heavy bank balance but with an active imagination. Bergdorf Goodman in New York, famous for its lavish window displays, once covered the entire back walls of its vast windows with burnt toast graded from light to dark, with stylishly dressed mannequins at the front. The windows should have cost no more than the price of some loaves of bread and a toaster, unlike the store's famed Christmas windows where huge amounts are spent.

There are a variety of ways to use and source props to achieve stunning window displays.

Opposite
Expensive and maybe not quite politically acceptable, but the use of a life-sized deer to display fashion accessories at Printemps in Paris is an example of the many exotic props that are available for hire.

Props en masse

An interesting way to introduce props to a window is to arrange them en masse. Acquire something cheap and easily available, such as an empty tin can, for example. By itself on the floor next to an item of furniture, it may look lost and bear no obvious relation to the window theme. Used en masse, however—possibly covering the wall or floor—the cans become a bold statement, just as stacking hundreds of bottles of the same perfume aesthetically changes the emphasis from product to prop, but cleverly uses the merchandise to do this.

Custom-made props

Handmade props will possibly incur some costs; however, they are generally worth the extravagance. If the visual merchandiser requires items made especially for a window scheme, he or she will either approach a prop-maker or make them personally. A professional prop-maker will take the brief away and develop the concept further; it is wise to see a sample to check for sizing/color/finish before committing to the final design. Only when the client is happy with the designs will manufacture of the finished design begin. It is always wise to use prop-makers who have an understanding of window displays, as they will know when to cut corners on the overall finish yet consider the project as a whole and deliver a finished prop on time, to a high standard, and within the budget agreed. Prop-makers will also be specialists in carpentry and paint finishes, and will also be able to work with many other materials. When briefing the prop-maker, it is worth remembering that a closed window will only require the prop to be finished on one side, as the back will not be seen from the street, but a prop for an open window will need to be finished on all sides so that it can be viewed from 360 degrees.

Build up a collection of generic props that can be reused and interchanged, or even carried into the store interior at a later date.

Above
These simple bust forms used en masse form a very powerful display, showing as it does the authority and range of a coat collection available in-store in Topshop, London. The simple slogan "COATS" also highlights the product.

Below
Used in a carefully constructed rectangle, these simple slate tiles displayed en masse in a Macy's New York window create a subtle support for the mannequin, which is itself dressed in neutral clothing.

Opposite
The clever use of rope en masse as a prop at Liberty's, London, is used to carefully suspend mannequins for a dramatic window scheme.

Fresh flowers are an effective way to promote a specific season.

Recycling props

Resourceful visual merchandisers will store props and use them again at a later date, possibly in the windows once more, but with a new finish or—more often than not—in the interior of the store. One should try to get as much mileage out of the props as possible, especially if they were costly. However, they should not be overexposed; the customer will expect to see something new. Remember that well-manufactured props can be used in-store at another time. Many visual merchandisers will shrewdly pick up items from junk shops and reuse them at a later date. It is worth remembering that large, overpowering props can only be used so often before the public begins to recognize them from behind the makeovers. Smaller discreet items, on the other hand, can be painted and decorated in many ways and used in a multitude of displays if interchanged with other props.

Flora

Flowers and plants can be very effective in a window presentation but they may not live long; the heat from the sun and also from the window lighting can wither even the healthiest of plants in just a few hours. Artificial plants have become much more realistic through the years, and can be cleaned, packed up, stored, and used again.

Getting the most from the props one chooses will not only help complete the window display but it will also make the job of a visual merchandiser a lot easier. It is always worth planning how and when to use props, as well as what they ultimately will contribute to a window display. A prop may have been costly and look good on paper, but always question if it is truly effective.

Above
The use of these artificial flowers brings a fresh, spring-like theme to this Topshop window in London, with the advantage that they will not wilt or die.

Opposite
Artificial topiary has been used on a bust form at Fortnum & Mason, London, to display ladies' fashion jewelry.

esigning a
indow display

Having chosen the merchandise, the theme, and the props, there are a few simple preparations a visual merchandiser needs to make to ensure that the window installation process goes smoothly.

Sketch

The first stage in designing a window is to sketch a proposed layout. Professionals will make a rough plan of how they want the finished window to look. These rough drawings are often not to scale, but they reassure the designer that the overall completed window presentation will work. Many visual merchandisers who are required to present their window schemes to third parties may need a detailed diagram drawn to scale. These two-dimensional visuals are usually created with the help of a computer-aided design program (CAD). An experienced CAD user can

produce a realistic suggestion of the window design. For beginners, a Photoshop program will suffice. Only the most experienced visual merchandisers can confidently enter a window and produce a work of art without a detailed diagram. The more hands-on experience gained, the less detailed the sketches will need to be. Tried-and-tested windows will always succeed.

Above
A simple, hand-drawn sketch that can then incorporate color and texture will give you an idea of the overall look of your window design. This particular layout is an example of pyramid grouping (see page 70).

1 The merchandise is grouped together to reflect the form of a pyramid.

2 A large vase helps to anchor the pyramid on the left-hand side.

3 This vase sits at the top of the pyramid.

4 A table on the right-hand side of the display creates optical balance with the vase on the left-hand side.

5 The use of two colors in the display helps to create a more dramatic image.

6 Eye level, also the focal point, as the window would be viewed by a passerby in the street, is slightly off-centre.

7 The display faces the street and is positioned in the center of the window to gain maximum attention.

8 CAD allows experimentation with different textures in the design, here allowing selection of the best wallpaper.

Above
A CAD version can be made to scale and used as a more professional means of presenting your window-display ideas to colleagues.

Below
Erwan and Ronan Bouroullec design for the window of Issey Miyake's Apoc store in Paris shows how CAD can be used to organize products in a window.

Layout

There are a series of rules and standards that the visual merchandiser should consider when laying out a window. However, like many professionals who rely on guidelines, experienced visual merchandisers often break them, either because they wish to be controversial or because they have the skill to know exactly how and when to leave tradition behind. Before novices bite off more than they can chew, however, it is always wise to understand the basic rules. Once this valuable knowledge is instilled in them, they will have a deeper understanding of the ethics behind designing a window and of how best to capture the public's attention.

Focal point

Large or small, a window needs to have a focal point on which, when viewed from the street, the eye will instinctively rest. Larger windows may need more than one. The focal point is best placed just below eye level, just off-center. The eye may then be guided around the window display to other products. Remember: if a window is higher than the pavement, the focal point will have to be lower. It is always best to view the window from outside to ascertain where the main focus should be. Customer flow will also affect the way the window is viewed. If the majority of pedestrians approach the window from the left, then the grouping should be aimed to the left; it would be a shame to spend valuable time planning and dressing a window only for the bulk of customers to notice the back of the mannequins, merchandise, or props.

Above
A typical pyramid grouping that can be used for both housewares and fashion. The focal point is the dark-red vase on the second shelf of the unit at the back, just off-center. It is important to make the focal point eye-catching.

It is unwise to position the main products or props on the side walls, leaving a large void in the center of the window, just as it is foolish to hang key items too high in the window, as the eye may be guided to the ceiling and thus out of the window.

Deep windows can be problematic. The visual merchandiser often positions product groupings toward the front of the glass, hoping that they will get the maximum exposure from the display. However, by placing some items at the front with more behind leading back to the wall, a customer's eye can be encouraged to follow the carefully positioned objects back into the window. This also applies to center displays with product trailing out toward the side walls.

Optical balance

Understanding the term "balance" when designing and installing a window display is essential. To a visual merchandiser, the composition of the window display relates to how the product is aesthetically balanced. Correct balance is achieved when the presentation shares equal optical weight. There are two main compositions: informal balance, known as asymmetrical, and formal balance, known as symmetrical. Both can be effective if executed correctly. Formal balance is easier to comprehend because the same objects are used to create a mirror image. Informal balance relies on the visual merchandiser using various objects but still creating an even distribution of the optical weight.

Using odd numbers is also a general rule when grouping products or mannequins. Three mannequins positioned tightly together will appear stronger than two.

Above
The first group in the illustration (top) shows two identical vases, which clearly balance. The second group (bottom), however, shows products that are different on each side of the shelf, but optically their weight is the same and so they also balance.

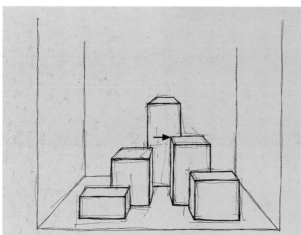

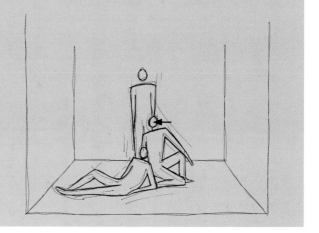

Groupings

Arranging products in an aesthetic way is referred to as "grouping." There are two styles of grouping commonly used: pyramid and repetition groupings.

Pyramid grouping

Any noted visual merchandiser who has been trained in the art of window display will be aware of "pyramid" grouping. For years, both in-store and in windows, this common rule has been practiced around the world. The idea is that both props and products create pyramids. Aesthetically, it is a proven way to group products together so that the eye focuses on one main point first and is then led on to other focal points around it. The pyramid also enables the eye to remain for longer on the key product that is being emphasized.

Above
The mannequins and props in this scheme by Harvey Nichols in London are used to create a pyramid grouping. The center mannequin is elevated by positioning her on the metal sculpture, which also adds drama to the scheme.

Below left
In this pyramid grouping the focal point is at the left-hand side of the second-largest box.

Below right
In the pyramid grouping, the focal point in this group of mannequins is the head of the central figure.

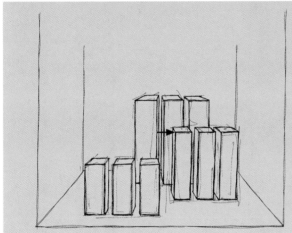

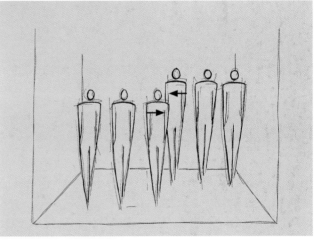

Repetition grouping

Repetition grouping is another interesting way of arranging products. This style of dressing sounds straightforward and simple; however, only the most talented of visual merchandisers can produce outstanding repetition groupings. It is easy to lose the focal point within a window with repetition; never assume that the centre prop will the be the focal point if it does not stand out enough to gain attention. A line of three mannequins may not have an obvious focal point, so sometimes you might have to work hard to create it using merchandise; thus, the jacket on the center mannequin could be

brighter or bolder and be used to navigate your eye into the window. Placing the bold jacket on the end of the run of five manne-quins may lead your eye to the side of the window and out. The aim is to use multiples of the same products to create a stronger presentation. Three perfume bottles will have more authority than one; 30 will undoubtedly have more impact.

On occasion, repetition groupings can be built up to create pyramids. Pyramid and repetition groupings generally do not work well together as the overall effect can look messy with no main focus or design aesthetic.

Above

Three male mannequins stand rigidly together to create a strong repetition grouping in this French Connection window in London.

Below left

It is harder to find the focal point in a repetition grouping. The different heights employed in this window by the three staggered blocks means that it naturally falls off-center on the left-hand side of the medium-sized blocks.

Below right

In this window, six mannequins are split into two groups, with three at the back and three at the front. Depending on whether you stand on the left or the right of the window, the focal point could change. From the left, it will fall on the third mannequin from the left in the front row; this is because the second row will be hidden behind the first. From the right, the focal point would be on the third mannequin in from the right in the back row. Both focal points need to be planned when dressing the window.

Store study:
Lane Crawford

Lane Crawford is the leading fashion store in Hong Kong for international designer brands. Founded in 1850, its stores are sited in various prime locations around the city. Bartley Ingram is the Visual Merchandising Director who is responsible for fulfilling the company's program for contemporary store designs and innovative visual merchandising to underpin the store's exclusive place in the field.

What was your favorite window that you designed?

"That's like trying to choose your favorite child! There have been many that I have loved for different reasons. Some because of their obsessive/compulsive properties, and some for their simplicity. If I have to choose a recent display, it would be for Azzedine Alaïa. We just had three mannequins in very chic garments,

all in black and white. We then spelled out 'Alaïa' on the floor with shoes from the brand. It was so simple, elegant and didn't cost a penny."

What is the hardest product category to design a window scheme for?

"The hardest category of products to design a window for is what I call 'smalls'. This includes cosmetics, jewelry, etc. It is so easy to put a fabulous outfit on a mannequin and you're done. It is much harder to focus on little things and get a big impact. It can be done easily in a little window, but it is trickier in a large space. What you need to do is make a broad statement that grabs people's attention from a distance, and then focus their field of vision onto the product by drawing them into the center, corner, back wall, or floor of the window to notice the little gem. Pin spotlighting and clever signage are a sure-fire way to get this done."

Whose other windows do you admire?

"I love all kinds of windows. There is a shop in Causeway Bay, Hong Kong, that sells fire extinguishers and they have the most amazing window. The back wall is black and they have about 25 fire extinguishers on pedestals, which are obsessively positioned according to their height. And I love pharmacy windows in Europe because of their attention to detail. They can be quite beautiful. And of course I get inspiration from Barneys, Dover Street Market, Loveless, and Colette."

How important is store design, does it help sell products?

"Store design is the canvas that display people paint on. It is the foundation. It makes our job so much easier if we have a gorgeous environment in which to create. A really good store is easy to navigate, friendly, has great

Above
The use of dramatic red boxes projecting from the walls is not only aesthetically pleasing but practical as they can hold products.

ALL BAGGED UP.

Above
For Christmas 2006 Bartley Ingram asked the artist Zoe Bradley to go to Hong Kong and create four special pieces out of paper for the store. The theme was "Christmas Unwrapped," and the featured dress was made entirely out of their red gift boxes.

RED CARPET MOMENT

music, is aesthetically pleasing, and has pockets of interest around every corner that leave you feeling as if you have had a real sensory experience as you exit. At Lane Crawford we have the good fortune to work with architects Yabu Pushelburg, who have created what I consider two of the most beautiful stores in the world for us in Hong Kong. Not only do they work with the most luxurious materials you could find around the globe, they also really understand designing a retail space that flows naturally and presents the merchandise in a way that makes it irresistible. They really understand the shopping experience and pay attention to every detail, from gorgeous, luxurious furniture, to spacious fitting rooms, to just the right lighting."

How does the store design help the visual merchandiser?

"Store design helps a visual merchandiser in the same way the best fabric mills in Italy help a custom tailor create the perfect suit. If you have the best fabric, you can make a beautiful suit. If you have a beautiful store, anything you do will automatically look better."

How important are signage and graphics both in store and windows?

"Signage is probably the most important component to any display. You can't assume that every person who sees a display is going to understand it. There are many ingredients that go into signage. It needs to educate, explain, and make the product something you just have to have."

Above
Zoe Bradley's Christmas paper designs are again used in this dress, creating a pleated piece where each sheet of Lane Crawford wrapping paper was meticulously folded. The mannequin is elevated on a plinth for greater effect.

Is good lighting both in store and windows key?

"My team gets so tired of me talking about lighting. I have taught them a little trick to remember the two most important things. Each time they do a display, they hold up two hands. Right hand equals signage, left hand equals lighting. If they have done both, they are finished."

What will store windows be like in 50 years?

"In 50 years, I am not sure we will even have store windows. Products might just be imagined by a designer and then show up at your door through osmosis. (If you have a door.)"

Whose mannequins do you like to work with most?

"Goldsmith in New York is our major supplier. We also work with Bonaveri in Italy and Beekwilder in the Netherlands."

Do you have any tips for in-store visual merchandising and windows?

"Understand the product you are displaying. Whether it is a handmade shoe, a face cream, or a piece of fine jewelry, if you get to know the product, the inspiration for the display is in there somewhere. It is about educating and exciting the customers about why they can't live without it."

Above
In a display to promote the concept of the "little black dress," black sparkly gift boxes are strung together with ribbons to extend the display across the ceiling.

Color

The use of color can create drama and atmosphere. Most retailers rely on color as an inexpensive tool to change the window's look and image. Color can be added in many ways, the most obvious being paint. Lighting, fabric, and graphics can also create impact.

Colors can be extremely personal; not everyone's tastes and preferences are the same. In different cultures, colors may mean different things. For example, pink is seen as the navy blue of India. Some colors have an almost global reference. Red is seen by many as a warning color, known to get one's heart racing; this is possibly why it is also the color used by most retailers at sale times, when they encourage a shopping frenzy by ensuring their customers literally "see red." The mint-green aprons that British surgeons wear are by no means a fashion statement; they are in fact colored that way because the eye will settle more easily looking at them after focusing on the color of blood—light green is calming. Many mental institutions color their walls with the same shade. With this in mind, it is worth considering the impact that color

can have on a customer looking at a window display.

Using the wrong colors can, of course, be detrimental to a retailer. The autumn/winter 2006 fashion collections, into which the major British chains bought heavily, struggled to sell because of their color: gray. Many women especially felt that the color was drab and hard to wear without looking dull. The visual merchandiser could have tackled this problem by complementing it with accessories, backdrop colors or an imaginative display.

It is useful for visual merchandisers to understand the basic principles of color and what effects they may have on their customers. The color wheel is certainly the most effective way of understanding how colors work.

Above
The use of red and gold in this window from Printemps in Paris gives a rich, warm feel to the window. Note how the rich pattern of the background is in harmony with the theme.

The color wheel

In the late seventeenth and early eighteenth centuries, Sir Isaac Newton created the very first color wheel. By use of a prism, he split sunlight into colors to create a color spectrum. A century later, the German writer Johann Wolfgang von Goethe produced his own version of a color wheel based on the psychological effect of colors, where reds and oranges were positive and greens to blues more unsettling.

The color wheel that is used today is based on three primary colors: yellow, red, and blue. When mixed together, these three colors produce every other color. By blending two of the primary colors, a secondary color is created: yellow and red mixed together will make orange, for instance. A primary color mixed with a secondary color will form a tertiary color: yellow and green, for example, create yellow-green.

Color terms

Chromatic

High color density: red, blue, and yellow.

Achromatic

The opposite of chromatic: gray, white, and black.

Shade

Adding black to a color will alter the appearance of the color and make it darker: a different shade of the original color.

Tint

Adding white to a color will brighten the color, creating different tints of the original color.

Hue

Another name for the pure color: red, blue, etc.

Value

The darkness or lightness of a color.

Above
The twelve colors of this color wheel consist of the three primaries, the secondary colors, and the tertiary colors.

Color schemes

To a novice visual merchandiser, exploring the use of color and determining what effects it can have in a display may at first be daunting. Co-ordinating colors so that they are effective should be considered thoroughly before designing or installing a display. The most common color schemes are based on just six variations (see opposite).

One of the most effective window schemes that has been used by visual merchandisers worldwide is the use of only one color. Various shades of the same color used in the same display can create impact. A window based on the color blue, for example, can add an emotional value; it could be perceived as cold, sad, or—depending on the hue—warm. By using the relatively inexpensive medium of paint on the walls in one shade of blue and adding mannequins in another shade and the product in different shades again, the window will look striking and will be cost-effective, too. Depending on the dressing and styling, color can also promote a trend: pink for Valentine's Day, for example; red for Christmas; or black for a more luxurious fashion look.

By painting the walls and floor in different colors, each will stand out to frame the product. It is also the perfect way to create a realistic room set.

Above
An achromatic window can be very effective and easy to design. Here at Selfridges, London, a solid black floor and checked wall help complement the contemporary furniture display in collaboration with "Elle Decoration."

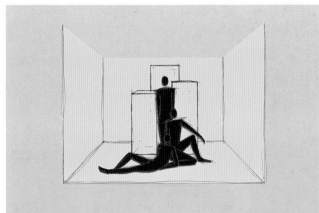

Complementary
Two colors that are directly opposite each other on the color wheel.

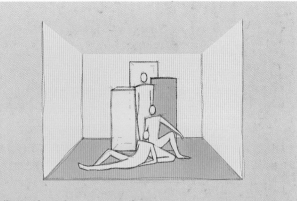

Split-complementary
The use of three colors: one main color and two colors appearing either side of it on the color wheel.

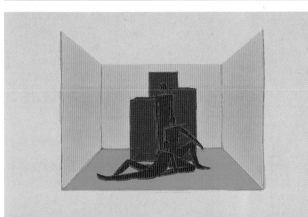

Double complementary
Four colors, two main colors plus their complementing hues.

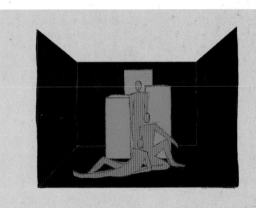

Triadic
Three colors that are all equally spaced around the color wheel.

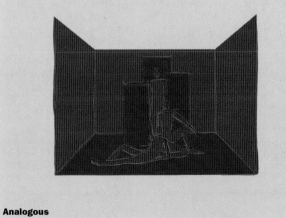

Analogous
Two or more colors that are next to each other on the color wheel.

Achromatic
Black and white.

Above
The use of color in a window display is paramount in its success. These examples demonstrate how color can be used as a useful tool for attracting the customer's attention.

Color really is the most magnificent tool for capturing the attention of passersby and creating atmosphere. If in doubt, always go for the brighter or darker option. Taking the soft option will not be as effective and will be perceived as predictable by the customer who may overlook the color scheme—cream instead of crisp white will appear weak, and the wrong shade of red may look like a sale window.

When using color, it also pays to consider the color associations behind the product itself. Whereas a window promoting eco-friendly products would benefit from the window being colored in neutral tones associated with natural products—ecru, cream, and off-white—a butcher would never use red as a backdrop for his products; instead he uses white because it will always appear hygienic and show off the cuts of meat. A jeweler specializing in diamonds will, of course, rely on a rich, dark color that will offset the gems and make them sparkle.

There are also tricks you can use with color to change the look of the window. A darker color such as black will make a large window appear smaller. White, on the other hand, will create the effect of space. Painting or applying vertical stripes to the window walls will visually stretch it.

Opposite
The mask in this window from Printemps in Paris appears to be floating against the black background, giving the complete window a real sense of drama. A large window painted black will make it appear smaller and also create great atmosphere.

Above
Painting stripes on a wall will make the window appear taller as well as create an interesting and economical wall treatment, seen here for the "Spring Beauty" display at Selfridges in London.

Below
Using different shades of blue products against a blue wall creates an effective theme at Printemps, Paris. An entire scheme was also created by using a different color for each window in a run of windows while maintaining the same layout.

Window prepping

Once it has been decided which products are to be used, it is wise to collect everything and prepare it beforehand. This will save valuable dressing time.

Preparing merchandise, or "prepping" as it is commonly known, will speed up the window-dressing process. Clothing can be selected in advance and ironed or steamed, price tags can be removed, and in some cases, manne-quins can be dressed away from the windows and added later. Fashion dressers may often require hosiery and other accessories; these should also be selected during the prep time.

Household goods can be picked and prepped: glasses cleaned, labels removed, and fabrics ironed. The more prepping that is done in advance, the less work there will be when a window is being dressed. Once the products are selected and prepped, they can be added to the window.

Above
In this Zara shop in Elx a group of mannequins stands in-store, mirroring the seasonal design of the window display, promoting the same message throughout both the windows and the store.

Above
The structural and architectural
theme running through this window
from Macy's in New York is part of a
larger scheme that not only ties the
windows together but also acts
as a generic backdrop for various
fashion looks.

Installing the window display

No retailer wants shop windows to be either empty or in a state of undress for long. It is therefore important that a feasible time slot is allocated to dress a window from start to finish. Unless the window scheme is complicated and needs to be dressed over a couple of days, a visual merchandiser should ensure that the window is completed in a day. Many visual merchandisers start early in the morning in order to strip out the existing window scheme while the store is closed so as not to hinder the customers by trailing props and products across the shop floor. It is also an easier time to bring the new scheme to the window.

If the window scheme has been planned accurately, the subsequent dressing of the window should be trouble-free. It is essential that the window about to be dressed is clean and neat; checks should be made to ensure all the lighting is working and that light bulbs have not blown out. It is easier to put up a ladder and replace light bulbs before the window is full. Staples, nails, and screws from the previous dressing will need to be removed

and, in many cases, holes in walls will need to be filled and sanded.

Next, the walls should be treated. The floor should be left for last in order to avoid unnecessary paint splashes. If the walls are to be painted, it is often wise to start very early in the day, as they may require several coats and, depending on the weather, they may take a long time to dry. Leaving the lighting on will also help raise the temperature by a few degrees. It is advisable to mask the edges of the glass close to the walls; paint-speckled glass will be noticeable to the customer. If the window has a solid floor such as marble or wood, this should also be covered to prevent paint splashes unless it, too, is being painted.

If the window has floorboards cut from MDF, they can be removed and covered away from the window while the walls are being painted, thus saving time. Covering large boards with either fabric or PVC can be difficult purely because of their size—assistance may be needed. As part of your toolbox (see page 200) a staple gun and a pair of scissors are a visual merchandiser's saviors; they will be

Above
The façade of Liberty's in London is impressive, but it also means the customer has to focus a little more on what is for sale in the windows. Planning a window scheme that can compete with the architecture is important.

required on many occasions, especially when covering panels. Always cut the fabric larger than the board, leaving enough spare to hold and pull while you staple. Start on the longest side first, putting a few staples in the middle of the board on both sides. Then do the same on the shorter sides, pulling the fabric taut; work toward each of the corners securing the fabric with staples as you go. When you reach the corners, fold the fabric neatly under the board and add some final staples. Remember: you may also need to strip the boards for the next window scheme, so try to use as few staples as possible. Removing staples can be time-consuming and arduous.

With the walls painted and the floors finished, the dressing can commence. It is always advisable to introduce the props first—they will be the backbone of the whole window scheme. Position the props where you think they will attract attention, remembering that the products should be king and that the props must interact with the merchandise. Larger props are generally placed toward the back of the window, with smaller ones toward the front. It would be pointless to hide the products (and any other props) with a bulky

prop. Any hanging props should be suspended first; they must be securely wired or fixed to the ceiling grid. Freestanding props can then be added and arranged.

Remember, mannequins are also props designed to support clothing. It is always worth considering where they will be positioned and how they will interact with the window scheme.

If the window is backless, the unappealing rear of a piece of furniture such as a cabinet will be in full view. Placing another cabinet backing onto it can hide the ugly side and can also be dressed to face in-store, giving the customer two chances to see the display: when entering and when leaving.

As with props, large products should be placed in the window first. It is important at this time to distribute the larger items so that they form the backbone of the main bulk of a grouping. A window may have many groupings, all trailing from one main grouping. The largest and main grouping should be made up of the largest item. A refridgerator, for example, could stand just off-center, with a grouping of other appliances around it; a

Above
Saks on Fifth Avenue, New York, used warm lighting that emits a glow from the windows in this scheme. In cold weather this can encourage shoppers into the store.

washing machine may be positioned to the left, near but not touching the refridgerator with another selection of electrical items; to the right of the window a microwave could be positioned with a smaller group of electrical accessories. It is important that the largest grouping is installed first, before the smaller ones. Concentrating on one small area of the window before finishing the bigger area is not advisable, because it is the fully completed window as a whole that should be considered as the sales device, not just one specific area.

Checking the window from street level is essential. Spending long hours dressing a window without looking at it from the customer's viewpoint can lead to problems: the focal point might not be in the correct place and the whole window scheme may need to be adjusted, thus wasting time.

Closed windows can be claustrophobic and sometimes get very hot. It is always best, not only for one's sanity but also for creativity, to take breaks from difficult dressings. A five-minute rest may inspire and initiate ideas.

When a window is 90 per cent complete, it is time to adjust the lighting. The lighting is one of the most vital elements of a window display and, sadly, one that many visual merchandisers forget to adjust. Hours can be spent dressing and perfecting a window

display, so it only makes sense to illuminate it to make it stand out to the passersby. A spotlight focused on an empty back wall can be very distracting—and at night, very visible.

Attention should be focused on the price tags, if used, to make sure that not only are they spelled correctly but that they are also positioned adjacent to the relevant products. It is also important to make sure that the text used is large enough to be seen from the street. Finally, all surfaces should be cleaned and floors should be swept.

Some stores have the luxury of having a mock window in the studio, complete with lighting rig, where a whole window can be installed and dressed to see if the design works aesthetically. Retail chains might use this as a visual tool, once photographed, for visual guidelines that can then be sent out to regional stores.

Above
In this Macy's window, New York, soil is piled into a window set with simple white walls to create a display with balance that does not overpower the mannequins.

Above
In this window at Harvey Nichols in
London, a prop made using reflective
metallic strips may dominate the
window but it does not overpower the
fashion. Time, effort, and money are
usually expended on props, so it is
worth ensuring that they will be visible.

Lighting

Paul Symes, the visual merchandising manager for London's Fortnum & Mason, has always had an obsessive interest in lighting and technical wizardry. His tips for ensuring a window is well lit are:

Ensure all lighting fixtures are cleaned and working before dressing a window.

While adjusting lighting, a simple way to see if the beam is focused on the correct product is to wave your hand in front of the lamp and see where the shadow falls.

Use lamps of the correct beam widths.

Have a supply of spare lamps on hand.

Check the window lighting during the day and at night.

Be certain that the light beams are aimed into the windows—not facing out toward the public, thus blinding potential customers.

Lighting should never be an afterthought. The process of lighting a window should be planned at the same time as the window scheme (see the Lighting chart on page 202 for assistance).

A track system with adjustable lights offers the most flexibility in windows and gives the visual merchandiser the opportunity to use several different lighting fixtures, each of which will perform a different role within the display. Spots will highlight an individual piece of merchandise or mannequin, while floods will give an ambient light to the whole.

The wattage and beam width of a light can be baffling to a novice. The actual fixture is useless without the correct light. Many lighting fixtures can take a variety of lamps, but not all of them will be universally effective. The size of the beam width you require usually depends on the size of the grouping it is expected to highlight. A small piece of jewelry,

Above
A detail from the Harvey Nichols scheme, also pictured opposite, shows how a narrow-beam pin spotlight can be used to highlight the mannequins, and in particular the make-up carefully co-ordinated with the theme.

for example, will only require a three-degree beam width; anything wider will illuminate the surrounding area. Large, deep windows may require flooding with a general wash of light before spotlights are used to highlight individual items. A run of windows should each have a similar quantity of light; a dark window placed in a run of ten will stand out for the wrong reasons, as will a bright window.

Color and the time of day also need to be taken into account when choosing lighting. Some colors absorb light and others will reflect it. If a light-absorbing color such as black or dark blue is being used, extra lighting may be required to compensate. Fabrics and carpet will also absorb a substantial amount of the lighting in a window.

Lighting used in the daytime can differ from the amount needed at night. In a bright window with the sun shining on it, more light will be required to compensate for the extra daylight. Less lighting, as strange as it may seem, is required at night because the windows will stand out against their dark surroundings—there is little other lighting with which they will compete. Many retailers have adopted a lighting system that can automatically adjust the lighting outputs, depending on the time of the day.

Above
Lighting adds drama to this Goth-themed window from Harvey Nichols in London. A spotlight is directed at the mannequin, while a wider beam is used to create a shadow on the back wall, and then another to light the background of the rest of the window.

Signage and graphics

There is no doubt that an illustration (graphic) or piece of text (signage) in a window is a sure-fire way to get a statement across to the customers, be it price-driven or informative. Many visual merchandisers not only use graphics to tell a message but also use them as part of their window schemes. The use of bold, colorful text can enhance many window displays. Often signage and graphics may be used as a statement to support the window theme, or sometimes as the prop that ties a window scheme together.

Signage

It is worth noting that too much information can be confusing and text should be used cautiously. It is rather arrogant to expect shoppers to read reams of text in a window. It is always best to keep any text simple and explanatory; punchy one-liners always work best. Window signage should be planned at the same time as the scheme or theme— it should never be an afterthought. Always consider how the signage interacts with the window scheme or products, and question whether the text enhances the window or if it is unnecessary. Any signage used in a window should always be prioritized in order of importance. A tag showing the price of an item of furniture may be more important to its sale than a sign stating its location in-store, while a banner offering a discount may overrule both. Either way, too many tags, signs, or graphics can lead to visual overkill.

The positioning of signage and the choice of color must be thoroughly planned before-hand. A green message carefully placed on the glass will not stand out against a green back wall; a contrasting color would work better. The same sign placed directly in front of the main grouping can either hide it or, if positioned correctly, draw the eye to it. Many retailers still place signage far too high in a window and expect the public to look up to read it. Positioning signage high in a window encourages the viewer's eye to leave the main focus of the window and trail off to the ceiling grid instead. The most common and conventional place for signage is at eye level from the street.

Graffiti, neon, TV screens and projected images may all be used to send messages to the public, and the same general rules apply. To get the message across, text must be clear and easy to read and digest.

Above left
Clever use of signage, in Saks of New York; suspended at an angle next to the mannequin, it creates an interesting yet inexpensive window scheme.

Above right
Part of a sequence of windows entitled "Spring Beauty" at Selfridges, London. The text is the theme that runs through each window, each caption relating to a recognizable quotation or colloquialism.

Above
Large-scale text is applied to the windows here to create not only a larger window scheme called "Shop Like a Man," but to also interact with the T-shirts on display.

Below
The text in this window—"Everything but the Kitchen Sink"—is an integral part of the display and is used to tie in the presentation of housewares with the larger scheme of "Spring Beauty."

Window signage

Window signage has progressed considerably over recent years. The once handwritten signs hanging from ceiling grids have been replaced with vinyl machine-cut letters that are usually stuck to the window glass. These state-of-the-art letters are accurately cut to a predetermined design by machine and can be produced in any color or typeface. Applying the text to the window, unfortunately, still has to be done by hand. There are many companies that will not only cut the signage for you but also apply it. The task itself is not difficult; however, patience will be required. One small slip and the lettering can fold back on itself and become ruined. The vinyl letters can be positioned on the outside of the window or inside. Both are suitable, although bored customers have been known to pick the letters off the outside of the glass.

To apply the letters, a piece of masking tape is placed on the non-sticky side of the text. This holds the text in its correct format and makes the whole line or word easier to handle. Before placing the text onto the glass, many professionals will spray the glass with a weak soapy liquid; the vinyl lettering is then placed on the glass and the soapy water allows the lettering to be adjusted. When the text is positioned in the correct place, a plastic squeegee the size of a credit card is used to press down the letters and force the water from between the adhesive and the window glass. Finally, the masking tape is carefully pealed off, leaving the text firmly stuck to the glass. When the text is no longer required, it can simply be scraped away with a sharp blade.

The same vinyl treatment can be applied to the entire glass, thus blocking off the window completely. As strange as it may seem that a book teaching the art of window dressing should encourage such an idea, there may be times when a retailer needs to spend days, not hours, re-dressing a window. Many large department stores will use this opportunity to maximize the value of their window space and inform the public of the new window scheme or promotion at the same time. The windows act as a temporary billboard and hide the disarray inside.

Above
Large, pink, translucent vinyl letters are used to project a message but not obscure the scheme behind. This window showing the history of Holt Renfrew from 1937, displayed in a large light-box of archival images, was part of a scheme in the store's flagship shop on Bloor Street, Toronto, Canada, promoting the company's re-branding as represented by six key attributes: aspirational, luxury, international, unexpected, heritage, and modern.

Descriptive signs

Descriptive signs are used to inform the customer of prices, location of products, or discounts. While many retailers prefer to be discreet and not inform the shopper of the price of an item, others proudly list the prices adjacent to the merchandise. When pricing the clothing on a mannequin, the sign should always read from top to bottom, listing the prices starting from the top as the mannequin is dressed: i.e. hat, shirt, trousers, shoes. The lettering should be large enough to be seen from outside the window and be positioned to the right of the mannequin. Each pricing sign in the window should be the same size and format. Some retailers use a Perspex stand to hold the sign, which can be purchased from display companies. Because of the static electricity in Perspex, however, such stands can act as a dust magnet and will need to be cleaned daily.

Merchandise can be priced in other ways, too. Smaller price tags may be pinned to clothing items, or housewares may have small signs placed among the groupings. Some items may need a description of the item to help the sale. An antique chair may require a brief history and list of the materials used in its construction; however, an edited version will suit most customers.

Handwritten signs are definitely frowned upon in the visual merchandiser's world; even the smartest handwriting will look unprofessional. A printed sign will always look better and be easier to read.

LO GO ™

Hat: $140

Jacket: $500

Knitwear: $300

Shirt: $250

Jeans: $220

Shoes: $360

Graphics

Photography, either displayed within or applied to the window itself, is now a common tool of the visual merchandiser. Modern digital technology has made large-scale photographic prints affordable and accessible. As well as being used in conjunction with the retailer's advertising campaign, images are often created specifically for a window scheme. Such graphics have the advantage of being easy to install—and, as they don't have to be stored, easily thrown away. Photographic images can be applied to heavy-duty paper or card and hung from the lighting grid, printed on vinyl and applied to the window, or printed on paper and stuck on the back wall. They can create an immediate window scheme that needs little advance planning and are quick to install. More than one skilled person will be needed to apply large-scale vinyl graphics to the glass. Care should be used in positioning them in the window. Ideally, they should not be applied to the side walls as they will only be seen by customers passing the window in one direction. Positioned on the back wall, however, they can be used to attract the eye into the window.

Above
French Connection's larger-than-life vinyl graphics dominate the façade of the London store and promote the season's trend.

Above
This impressive approach uses the
store brand as part of the building's
design at Uniqlo in Tokyo.

Window calendar

Large retailers will plan their window schemes well in advance using a window calendar. A well-planned window calendar will help a visual merchandiser organize window installation dates, ensure that each window has a scheme planned well in advance, and in many cases, will help with budget allocations. In a reassuring sense, it will also help the visual merchandiser's job run smoothly. It is highly likely that a window calendar will be amended throughout the year; promotions can run longer than anticipated, and unexpected new products often have to have windows dedicated to them. However, a tentative plan will add some structure to the process.

A window calendar is also a useful tool by which to communicate the workload for the year to others in the business. The buyers will want to ensure that the products that are to

be promoted arrive in time. The sales staff will also want to make sure they have enough back-up stock available in their departments.

For decades, a visual merchandising manager would plan a window calendar using seasonal events as a backbone. In Christian countries, November and December would be blocked out to promote the festive season; discounted sales would (and still do) domi-nate for two months in the year in winter and summer. Easter, Mother's Day, and Valentine's Day are just a few occasions that often have window schemes dedicated to them. It might appear thoughtful to remind the public of such events, but it can also be naive to dedicate a run of costly windows to an occasion that only lasts one day and might only generate sales of low-priced items such as greeting cards. Instead, it would be better to promote gift-giving occasions that might encourage sales.

Today, however, with the greater competition among retailers, product promotions usually supersede many of the traditional seasonal events. With this in mind it is advisable to be aware of which new product ranges have been bought by the buying department and when they are going to appear in store. Timing is critical for maximizing sales. It would be senseless to design a window scheme to promote new season collections if they are not present in the host department. At Selfridges, Alannah Weston prefers not to commit her windows to a year of schemes in case the fashion world dictates a new trend. "We work on only a six-month calendar because we like to keep the customer up to date with the fashion trends," she explains. "I do not like to commit to something a year away that might not be so topical when it finally arrives. If you plan too far in advance you can miss the point. We are a fashion business, whether it is apparel or home, and

Above
London's Fortnum & Mason traditionally presents elaborately themed Christmas windows. In this scheme, the front windows of the Piccadilly Street store were dominated by the tale of *Alice in Wonderland*. When the Christmas windows are dismantled in January, department stores usually start to plan the windows for the following Christmas. This allows time for research and design and the manufacture of props.

Above
This Christmas window from Harvey
Nichols in London features snowflakes
to produce a festive display.

we need know what is out there in the fashion world. Attending the fashion shows is a great inspiration for me. Christmas, on the other hand, because of the vast amount of work involved, is planned a year in advance."

In the twenty-first century, many retailers now acknowledge global traditions and beliefs. Retailers may not only attract new customers by promoting them but prove that they, too, are worldly and aware of cultural differences. A Chinese New Year window or a Diwali window may also break the traditional appearance of a company's window displays.

An annual window calendar can start at any month of the year. Many retailers like to begin with Christmas, because those windows usually take the most planning and may need to complement the in-store seasonal decorations. Certain dates may be fixed and unable to move. It is always best to add these first to structure the calendar.

Once the proposed dates are added to the calendar, the task of designing relevant window schemes to support them can begin. To make things easier, the store windows should be numbered; the window numbers

can then be set against the dates. The visual merchandiser will thus be able to check at a glance on what date windows 1 and 2 are to be re-dressed, for instance. Large stores may have numerous windows that may not all be dressed with the same window scheme. Windows may be split up to accommodate several promotions, and numbering the windows will clearly define the window allocations. A comprehensive window calendar will also show precisely when an existing window is to be stripped and the time allocated to install a new one. Remember: the less time the window is in a state of undress, the better. Window-removal dates should be considered while preparing the calendar.

Above
Thought has gone into which products should be featured in this Harvey Nichols window in London. Womens-, mens-, and childrenswear are all shown in a family setting that appeals to the Christmas shopper.

Structuring a window calendar

Decide how long you want your calendar to run: six months or 12? Many retailers will even use an 18-month calendar.

Decide how you wish your calendar to appear. Many visual merchandisers will use a paper chart, yet others may use a computer program that can be accessed throughout the business. An interesting calendar can be produced using images and designs to demonstrate how the window schemes appear in reality over the allocated time.

Allocate windows for major promotions first: i.e. Christmas and sale.

Add secondary promotions: i.e. Easter, Mother's Day, Valentine's Day.

Use the free window spaces to introduce window schemes that may be product-related: i.e. new season collections.

Discuss with the buying/ marketing team if they require window space to promote new departments or special events.

Allocate budgets to each of the window schemes. Remember that Christmas windows may justifiably attract a larger slice of the budget because they are generally in for longer and because the store may wish to compete with its rivals in major shopping areas— every store wishes to be noted for outstanding window displays at this time of year. Smaller schemes that are not in for a long time should not have large budgets set against them.

Design and plan the windows well in advance. Large schemes with complex props may need a lot of attention. Prop-makers have to be briefed and their studio time booked.

Always plan the removal of existing window schemes. On most occasions this should only take a couple of hours; however, complex displays may take longer and eat into your dressing time.

Completed windows can be photographed for reference later. This is best done at night with a black screen so that you won't get reflections. If you are a freelancer, take at least a quick snapshot for your portfolio.

Above
Lane Crawford, Hong Kong, takes on a more contemporary and populist view with its "Christmas Rocks" display.

Window standards and maintenance, and budget

To a few visual merchandisers it may come as a relief to have completed the task of dressing a window. Often they will not take note of their work again until weeks later, when they are stripping it, ready for the next installation. However, this attitude toward their work will never gain them a good reputation.

Standards and maintenance

Window checks are laborious and time-consuming, but they are essential for maintaining the standards of a window display. Senior visual merchandisers often delegate this task to their juniors. Window checks should be completed early in the morning and at the end of the day. A notepad and pen and a scrutinizing eye are usually the only requirements. A checklist can be produced to ensure that any member of the visual team will look for the same problems or mistakes.

The most common faults include the following:

Dust and dirt

Materials that hold static electricity, such as Perspex, will attract dust. There are sprays available that promise to help slow the build-up of dust; however, they will not prevent it. Surfaces and floors should also be checked for dirt and dust.

Fallen props and product

Not only should the visual merchandiser check for obvious problems such as a fallen mannequin, he or she should also look for props that may have moved or slipped. Adhesive glues can either dry out or melt in the heat of the window, dislodging materials or fabrics.

Fabrics

Draped fabrics can start to sag and begin to lose their effect after time in the window, and it is sometimes necessary to refresh them by adjusting and re-pleating. Colored fabrics can also fade in the sunlight; it is advisable to replace them if this happens because the faded color might be misleading to a customer.

Plants and foliage

Whereas artificial plants might look realistic to the consumer, dusty leaves will be a sure giveaway. The leaves can be washed or wiped down with soapy water. Fresh flowers must be monitored at all times, depending on the fragility of the blooms; petals will drop and stalks will wither.

Lighting

It is always advisable to scrutinize not just the dressing but the lighting too. Light bulbs often blow out and can leave parts of the window in shadow. In some cases whole lighting tracks can short-circuit. Lamps and chandeliers used in the grouping may also need light bulbs replaced.

Heat

The heat from the sun combined with the window lighting will often melt candles. To prevent this, cut the candles as short as possible; without the length and the weight, they are unlikely to droop.

Linda Hewson is Selfridges' visual merchandising window manager. Over the years, she and her team have produced many stunning displays that are often controversial and eye-catching. Here is her checklist for novices wanting to produce a successful window presentation:

Beginners should begin planning their window by understanding the concept or design thoroughly and the budget available.

- -

Always produce a visual or sketch before starting to install any products or props.

- -

Consider the space you have and what is physically possible; will everything fit through the door?

- -

Decide where the main focal points are going to be.

- -

Think about what products you will be representing. Whom are you targeting and will the products be suitable?

- -

Ensure that the props do not overshadow the product.

- -

Be certain that any mannequins being used are sympathetic to the product.

- -

Is it necessary to use graphics or signage?

- -

Choose a strong color palette.

- -

If using props, ensure that they are made to a high standard and are finished well.

- -

Remember: often the simplest windows are the best.

Budget

Spending vast mounts of money on visual merchandising will only benefit the store if the visual merchandiser has the expertise to demonstrate effective visual merchandising. Expensive props and elaborate window schemes still need to be installed and dressed by individuals who understand the fundamental rules of layout and how best to use the space to create stunning displays.

Having said that, setting a budget against a visual merchandising project is a necessary part of the process. Remember, it does not always cost a lot to be creative. Many of the most effective window displays have been economical yet effective.

When setting a budget, it is often easy to overlook the main factors that will eat into your allocated amount of money; painting a window, for example, may cost more than expected when you take into account the cost of the paint, tools, and painter. Signage and graphics can also be costly. Window-display projects may also require additional help from outside experts such as freelance dressers, and in these cases fixing a daily rate will help keep the work within budget. Of course, savings can always be made; a shrewd visual merchandiser will rarely discard used props or fixtures, as many can be recycled and reused (see page 66).

The future

The future of window displays lies in the hands of the retailers. Selfridges' Alannah Weston believes that the public will never stop admiring windows and will continue to visit major shopping areas for inspiration. "More and more, we need to open up our stores so that people can see in," she says. "That will obviously have an effect on the window displays of tomorrow; we are going to have to be very clever in how we approach it. Window displays, as in three-dimensional presentations, are always more effective than any plasma screen or two-dimensional presentation that I've seen; however, we have just recently seen a demonstration of a hologram machine that was very effective. If technology gets good enough, then we will use it—we are, after all, at the forefront of window displays. It's the same principle as questioning whether people will stop going to the theater when they can get movies on DVD. The experience and tactile nature of creative windows will always be more rewarding to view. Live models, movement, and definitely sound is something that I would like to use in the windows. However, all of that will only serve to support the original art of window dressing that has been around since stores opened."

Store study:
Fortnum & Mason

In 1705 Hugh Mason owned a small shop in St James's Market, London. By 1707 he had been joined by his lodger, William Fortnum, and together they started a business that has lasted 300 years. Throughout the centuries, Fortnum & Mason has built up a reputation as the purveyor of fine foods and groceries, not only with members of the British royal family but also with a loyal clientele, all of whom who appreciate exquisite food. As Charles Dickens wrote of one trip to watch the horse race known as the Epsom Derby, "Look where I will...I see Fortnum & Mason. All the hampers fly wide open and the green downs burst into a blossom of lobster salad!"

The challenge for the visual merchandising manager at Fortnum & Mason is to not only create inspirational windows but to do so while keeping the shop's tradition in mind.

Paul Symes has the task of producing the F&M windows. His "Cabinets of Curiosity" window scheme for December 2006 lived up to the grandeur expected. Here, Paul talks about the inspiration, creation, and installation of the F&M windows.

Fortnum & Mason has a very eccentric, unique quality. How did you decide on the window scheme?

"Fortnum & Mason houses a veritable feast of delights, sourced from far-flung corners of the globe. In a similar way in the eighteenth century, the appetite for knowledge led aristocrats to travel the world in search of undiscovered and interesting artifacts and objects, which they would then display in showpieces called 'cabinets of curiosities.' Eventually the cabinets would become as diverse and eccentric as the artifacts they held.

I wanted to produce a scheme that not only conveyed the eccentricity of the store but also allowed us to display an eccentric mix of product from all over the store. The cabinet of curiosities seemed to present the ideal showcase.

The cabinets had to be individual in themselves, with their own 'personalities,' but at the same time they could not overpower the product that was to be displayed in them. They not only had to have shelves and features to group product upon but also had to contain the displays within a specific area."

How important is it to keep the Fortnum & Mason brand image in mind while designing the window scheme?

"The brand image is of paramount importance when designing a window scheme; the scheme should not only sit comfortably with the brand image but also embrace it. This

Above
This style of casual grouping is used to maximize the space in the cupboard's shelves and drawers while retaining a focal point: the open drawer in the center.

Above
Fortnum & Mason's "Cabinets of Curiosity"-themed windows were used to
display an eclectic mix of food and fashion.

knowledge influenced my decision to create this 'eccentric' window scheme."

How long did it take for you to design and develop the window scheme?

"The design stage took a couple of days. Once I had thought about the initial concept, I then began to put my thoughts on paper in the form of simple sketches. I wanted to ensure that there was a common relationship between each cabinet, and that they sat comfortably alongside each other.

Then I drew more elaborate sketches, and began to add subtle details such as color and embellishment. The whole process took about a week."

How did you specify the windows for the prop-maker? How did you get your vision across to the prop-maker of how the windows should look?

"Initially we spent some time discussing my vision and feel for the scheme, but to a large extent the prop-maker worked from my original drawings. I wanted the scheme to sit comfortably with the products that would be displayed on the units, so we spent some time walking around the store looking at merchandise."

What was the process of getting the window scheme made after you had briefed the prop-maker?

"As soon as the scheme went into production, I started making weekly visits to the production studio. This was my first scheme for Fortnum & Mason, so it was important that there were no nasty surprises on installation day. Each stage of the manufacture was monitored and approved; sample paint finishes and embellishments were also discussed and approved.

During each visit I would take photographs of the props so that we could talk on the telephone between visits, with each party having a full knowledge of the detail under discussion."

What do you consider when selecting the merchandise for the windows?

"Prior to selecting products for the windows, I hold a briefing session for all the store's buyers. This usually takes the form of a visual

Above left, top to middle
A hand-drawn sketch is produced as an initial idea. A more detailed drawing is produced to scale to ensure that the scheme fits comfortably within the dimensions of the window.

Top right to below
The window prop is near completion and has one final check before the paint, gilding and decoration are applied. The completed tree growing out of the top of the cabinet adds a surreal note to the final window display.

presentation showing the development of the concept from the initial sketches through to the latest production stages.

During the following few days I visit each buyer to discuss the merchandise they wish to offer from their department, and start to work out how each product will feature in the windows, and I collect sample products to show the visual team. I then start to build up a mental picture of how the final windows will look: what color will be prominent, what the secondary color will be, and the style of dressing we will use."

How do you start the dressing process? Do you brief your dressing team beforehand?

"As soon as I have a clear picture in my mind of how the windows will look, I arrange for a briefing meeting with my team. At the meeting I will present the concept and show them the props, which will now be in the final stage of production. If time permits, some of the team may have visited the prop-maker and have seen the production themselves. I always dress the first window, usually with

a member of the team assisting. The majority of the products for the window will have been chosen and cleaned beforehand, but as with all things creative, there are always ideas that suddenly come to mind on the day."

Can you describe briefly the installation and timings of the window scheme?

"The design stage takes about a week. From there the production stage takes six weeks, and the installation of the props takes a day. It usually takes four days to dress a window run (eight windows) including lighting.

I like the scheme to simply arrive and be put into place. I don't want passersby to see empty windows but something magnificent even before we have started to add the product. To achieve this, the scheme is usually installed on a Sunday morning, and the windows are cleaned, ready for dressing first thing on Monday."

How important is the window lighting?

"Lighting can either make or break a window scheme, and very effective results can be achieved with inexpensive equipment. The most important rule is that it must be maintained and properly adjusted.

We have two basic systems in our windows: a high-level track with halogen wide and narrow spot beams for overall lighting, and a low-level track with low-voltage 20-watt narrow-beam spots for feature lighting. Occasionally we may use colored lamps, gobo projectors, or LED lights with changing effects. Each one of the fittings has an integral dimmer switch."

How do you maintain the windows to ensure that they remain fresh?

"The windows are checked and maintained morning, lunchtime, and evening, and cleaned on a daily basis. That includes any dust that may have accumulated overnight. They are re-dressed every two weeks with new products. If the same person passes our windows on their way to work each morning and again each evening they have seen the same display at least ten times in a week, which can seem like an age! I want people constantly to see something new, something that catches their eye. Our windows are never finished; they have always just begun."

Above
The lighting emphasizes the product with pin spotlights used to highlight the three main groupings.

In-store
Visual
Merchandising

"It is extremely important that we have an established theme that begins with our windows and translates to all areas in-store nationally. The in-store areas are just as important as our windows and provide our customer with information and entertainment."

John Gerhardt, Creative Services Director, Holt Renfrew

In-store visual merchandising is the process used to lead customers through a shop in a logical order, encouraging them to stop at designated points and, hopefully, to make a purchase. Ask shoppers why their favourite store should stand so high in their estimation and many will probably explain that the space is easy to shop in, the product is simple to find, and the signage is clear and informative. Each of these answers demonstrates effective in-store visual merchandising.

As a visual merchandiser, your input into the merchandising of the store will vary depending on the type of shop in which you are working. In a small boutique, you may be called upon to refresh the layout in order to encourage customers to browse, and you will have a great deal of input into how this is done. With a big chain, you will be more likely to be following directions from head office, which will often relate to buying programs, store promotions, and seasonal events. Specialist stores may rely on the visual merchandiser working with the buyers to arrange the floor according to the new season's products and trends. Whichever type of store you are in, the same disciplines of in-store merchandising will apply.

The key to successful in-store visual merchandising is a successful floor layout. First you need to establish product adjacencies before you can start to plan your floor layout. There is then a series of options from which you can choose your fixtures, as well as some basic rules of product handling to help you display your merchandise effectively. Trend areas and in-store displays, and point of purchase and add-on sales will help merchandise your shop. Signage and graphics can also help in-store visual merchandising, as can the creation of ambience. Finally, care and attention need to be given to maintenance standards.

Above

A range of visual merchandising tools, including linear and mid-floor fixtures, brand signage and mannequins, helps customers navigate Harrods' menswear floor in London.

Below

Not only has Lane Crawford, Hong Kong, created strong focal points to attract the customer on this men's floor but it has also added footprints on the floor to help guide the customer toward them.

Product adjacencies

The starting point is product adjacencies. This refers to which products sit next to each other: hosiery next to lingerie, kettles next to toasters, and fruit next to vegetables. To maximize the space and use of the selling floor, the customer should be guided through the fixtures and aisles from one product to the next. By placing products that have empathy with each other, customers will not get confused and possibly pick up other items for which they may not have specifically been shopping. Clever use of product adjacencies will reinforce the appearance of the area and give it authority. A handbag fixture positioned next to scarves, gloves, hats, and purses suddenly becomes an accessory department.

Making a rough plan

Before starting to lay out a floor, always check which product categories and brands are available to you to merchandise. The best and most effective way to start is by making a list. Taking a floor plan and tentatively noting where the products should sit will make the task more manageable. As well as product adjacencies, you might want to think about the location of strong product categories or key brands, which should ideally be positioned in prime locations. These brands and products will help the customer gain awareness of what the store, department, or space is selling and reinforce the strength and quality of the merchandise on offer. A wall of denim with strong branding, like Levi's for example, will make a statement and guide the consumer to the area where other brands of jeans are for sale. In the same way, a wall of pillows will inform customers that they are approaching the linen department.

As well as product adjacencies and the use of merchandise to guide the customer around the store, the other area to consider is customers' comfort level. A boutique selling both men's and women's clothes could have the two ranges merchandised together. Yet men might feel uncomfortable browsing through women's clothes to find their own; therefore a sensible approach might be to split the shop in two and dedicate one area for menswear and one for womenswear. The two areas would have to meet somewhere, and at this point the cash desk could be used to divide them, or you could feature products that could be classed as unisex, such as magazines, jewelry, or T-shirts. Getting the product adjacencies incorrect could be costly to the store and also drive customers away.

Finally, if you are positioning name brands, it is best to understand where they see themselves on a floor plan. Large brand owners may have very strong views and have the clout to exercise them. Egos can clash when dealing with prestigious brands which will expect prime locations; their demands should never be overlooked. Many smaller brands, on the other hand, often wish to be placed adjacent to brands to which their customers aspire.

Once you have placed the product categories and brands roughly on the floor plan, you should visually walk the shop floor; the aim is for your eye to follow naturally from one category to the other.

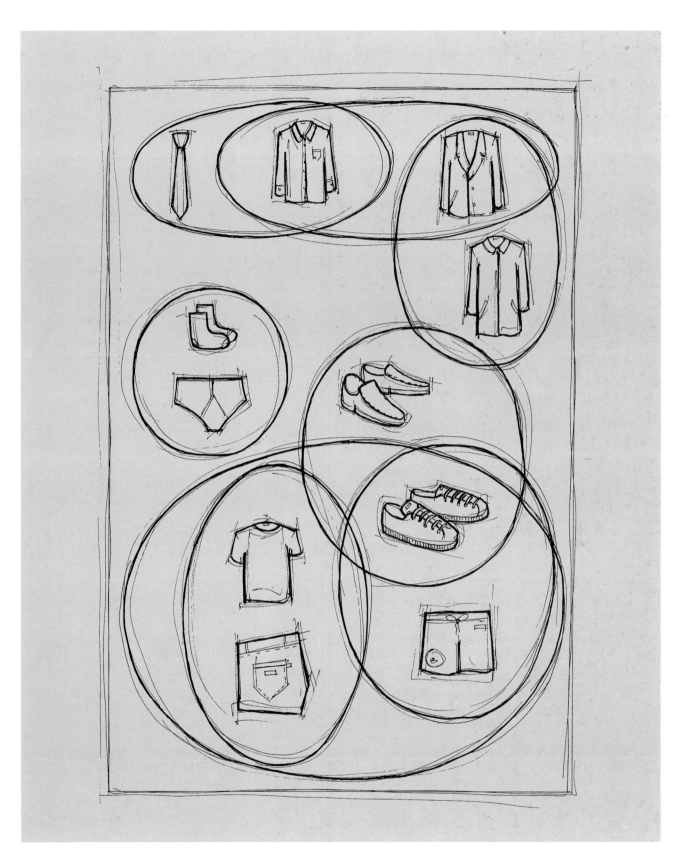

Above

Making a rough plan of the products that should sit next to each other is the first step in laying out a shop floor. This is called making the product adjacencies. Ties, jackets, and suits or socks and underwear are two examples. Eventually, all the groups of product adjacencies will interlink to create one cohesive floor plan that contains them all.

Floor layouts

Once you have noted your product adjacencies, it is now time to plan your detailed floor layout. Any shopper who is struggling to navigate the labyrinth of an IKEA furniture store will have noticed how difficult it is not to be tempted to leave the designated route. Once the customers have entered the store they have no choice but to traverse the shop to find the exit; while doing so they are led through numerous lifestyle room settings designed to offer inspiration, and then to a warehouse to spend. Even while standing in line, their children can enjoy an ice cream. Few people will understand the ingenious planning that has gone into creating such a disciplined floor layout.

Similarly, the countless aisles of shelves in a supermarket have been rigorously planned. While they may not inspire the customer, they do achieve their aim by making the monotony of grocery shopping effortless and uncomplicated. The exact location of the dairy products in relation to the cleaning products, for example, would have been carefully planned, not only to assist the customer but also to drive sales. Staples such as milk and eggs are not always placed at the front of a supermarket for the customer's convenience; they are often located in the center of the store or toward the back, ensuring that the shopper has to pass other items before discovering them. While searching, shoppers will probably add additional products, for which they were not necessarily shopping, to their baskets. Even the ends of the fixtures are used to make extra sales, often being used to promote offers. These invaluable spaces are usually placed along a central walkway with heavy traffic, making them a useful commodity to grab the shopper's attention—and money.

Each of these examples proves the power and effectiveness of a well-planned floor layout.

Above
Clearly defined walkways create ample space for shoppers to browse on the Marks & Spencer women's fashion floor.

Opposite
Milan's Corso Como features an eclectic mix of old and new furniture to display its products. Quirky lighting and art adorning the walls also help create atmosphere.

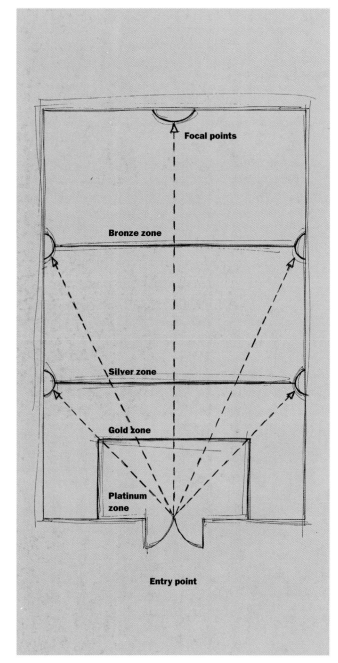

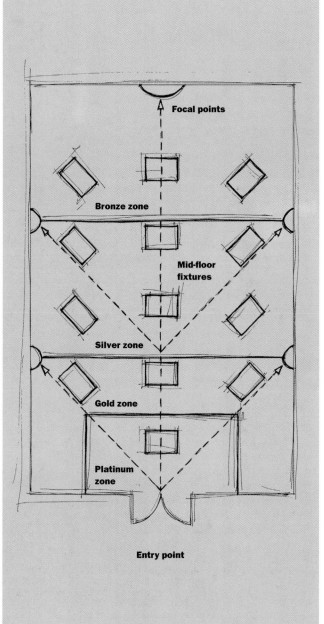

Above left
The floor layout here clearly shows the most profitable platinum selling space inside the entrance to the store. This area will be expected to take the most money, followed by the gold, silver, and finally bronze areas at the rear of the store.

Above right
The same floor layout is shown here with fixtures in place. Each fixture is angled at 45 degrees to funnel customers into the store. Fixtures are also placed in line with displays on the side walls, which create focal points that are also designed to attract customers into and through the store, encouraging them to explore the whole shop.

Platinum, gold, silver, and bronze areas

Key to laying out a floor is the positioning of products. Visual merchandisers often divide the floor into four areas and define these by colors: platinum, gold, silver, and bronze (other retailers may use numbers or letters). It is important to comprehend that the first area of the store when entering is the prime selling space; this is why it is called the platinum space. The second as you walk through the shop is called the gold area, the third toward the back of the store is silver, and finally the area at the back is bronze. The first thing to note on your floor plan is, therefore, the entrances, as they will determine where the customers enter and exit the store and thus the position of the platinum area. The lower-priced, sale, promotional, or high-fashion items should then be positioned in the platinum area. This is because the platinum space will always attract more customers and more sales. The bronze area at the rear of the store will draw fewer customers because of the distance from the main entrance, so with this in mind, it is best to place some staple products or a desirable product category there to encourage customers through the store.

In addition to using product placement to attract customers into and through the store, the most significant consideration when laying out a floor is to lead the customers through the platinum part of the store to the designated points where they can be encouraged to browse and spend. If this is done, customers will remain longer in the store, and the longer customers are in the store, the higher the chances that they will make a purchase. In order to keep them content, their shopping experience should be both trouble-free and enjoyable. Clear directions and walkways will guide them and good product presentations will help them decide what to buy.

A strong brand will act as an anchor to a floor and pull potential customers into a particular area of the store.

Above
An elevated view of the same floor layout looking in from the entrance. This shows how the eyes should easily focus first on and then through the fixtures to rest on the focal points.

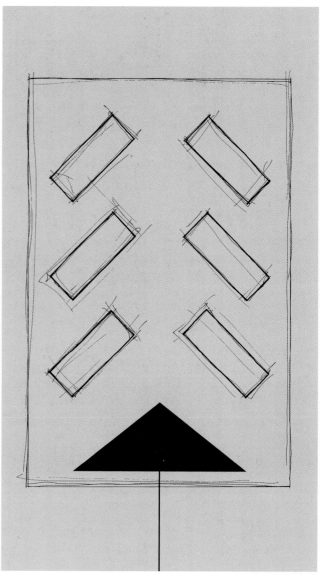

Chevroning is useful on large floors where there is plenty of space. In smaller stores, however, keeping all the fixtures straight and square to the walls will create the illusion of space.

Footfall, walkways, sight-lines, and focal points

A key factor that should be considered before laying a floor out is "footfall." This term refers to the route a customer walks through the store—or preferably the route the retailer wishes them to follow.

On entering a store, customers will be challenged with several decisions: do they go left, right, or straight, or decide to leave? Assuming that they stay, it will be the retailer's task to help them choose which way to walk around the store. Sight-lines and focal points will encourage them to explore the shop.

Sight-lines are imaginary lines that lead the customer to certain areas or specific products. Focal points can be an in-store display, a collection of carefully arranged merchandise, or a display featuring a key brand that immediately catches the eye. A focal point is best used in conjunction with the sight-lines. Once the customer's eye has followed a sight-line, it should comfortably rest on a focal point. It is therefore important that sight-lines are not obscured by large fixtures or walls.

Above

In the first illustration, the fixtures are placed in regimented rows at right angles to each other. This type of arrangement can form a barrier, discouraging customers from moving through the store. By moving the fixtures to a 45-degree angle, as shown in the second illustration, they can be used to funnel customers through the store. This is often called chevroning.

Above

Two fixtures placed parallel to each other do not encourage customers to view the in-store display and thus walk further into the store.

Below

By angling the fixtures, the mouth of the aisle is wider, funneling the customers toward the display.

Customers may be steered through the fixtures by defined walkways that act as sight lines. Many of these paths are designed to stand out physically from the rest of the floor, either because they are a different color or are made from a different material from the rest of the flooring. However, such defined walkways can also act as a barrier; many nervous shoppers subconsciously do not like to leave the comfort of the walkway. It is for this reason that it is possible to have walkways that are not defined; many stores have one universal floor covering, and cleverly position the fixtures to funnel the customers through the store. Fixtures or tables should, however, not be positioned so that they become obstructions or barriers. They should also be placed far enough apart that strollers, wheelchairs, or other mobility aids can be maneuvered easily between them.

Another feature that can be used to attract customers into and through a store is the walls. Linear (wall) space is a vital part of any shop. The walls surrounding the store can hold a vast number of products without eating up valuable shop-floor space. If key brands or strong product categories are positioned on linear fixtures, then the customer will see them and walk through the store toward them.

Above
In another form of floor layout, the lack of a defined walkway is counteracted by the use of fixtures to break up the floor space and create customer flow.

Positioning the products

With the above techniques for attracting customers into and through the store in mind, and referring to a product adjacency list, you can now start to lay out the floor plan and decide where best to place the products. Always start by placing the largest categories and key brands first: they will undoubtedly take up the most space and, hopefully, generate the most sales. With the adjacencies in mind, the next step is to fill in the gaps. One key factor to remember when doing so is the need to vary the pace—to create gaps between products or to introduce a different type of fixture, for example. This will keep the customers' attention, preventing them from becoming bored if every rack of clothing looks the same, or even overwhelmed if there is just too much crammed into the space.

Above
The prominently delineated red walkway has been designed to steer customers to the back of the store.

Sofas and armchairs, although a welcoming gesture, are a luxury as they do use up valuable product space.

Overall style of the floor layout

The style of the store's layout will depend on the products you are selling and what feel you wish the store to have. A designer boutique specializing in expensive garments may justify a spacious contemporary feel with minimal dressed fixtures. A women's clothing store may benefit from a feminine feel, while a men's clothing store may work better with harder lines and darker colors. A gift shop may lend itself to a more densely filled emporium with fixtures placed closer together. In this case, the key is to give the appearance of a generously filled store without making it look clumsy and busy. Large fixtures are best positioned toward the perimeter walls unless they are specifically designed to break up an area. Tables also can be a useful addition if they are merchandised correctly (see page 129). If you are using the walls to house branding or signage, it is important that it does not encroach into important linear selling space and that it is relevant to the product either beneath or in front of it.

Display areas should also be considered when planning the floor layout; remember that an in-store display may look appealing, but it will take up precious retail space. A group of mannequins might not get the same monetary return as a table of seasonal products. It is always wise to question if the floor is taking

on more of the resemblance of a showroom or museum than a shop. Customers will not interact with the products if they feel they should not touch them. Attaining the right mix of fixtures to display is essential in creating customer comfort.

Finally, consideration should be given to the cash desks and changing rooms. If they have not already been positioned, think about placing a cash desk at the back of the store in the least profitable area (bronze). This is not only a commercial decision, but will act as a tool to draw customers into and through the store. Changing rooms are also best sited at the back of the store. Stores with particularly attractive and portable merchandise that may be stolen will benefit from having cash desks at the front of the store as well as toward the back. Although there are no guaranteed ways of preventing shoplifting, positioning staff at the main exit may act as a deterrent.

Store study:
Atelier 1

Atelier 1 is based in Kiev, showcasing Ukrainian designers and their signature brand, Comme des Garçons. David Foley, who is the creator and founder, took his inspiration from his own home to theme the high-fashion store. His passion for antiques and couture is evident.

Your store has a very strong individual style. Can you explain the theory behind it?

"As an independent retailer, the opportunity to create a destination landmark was upper-most in our minds. We wanted to create the best possible international cutting-edge environment that would be a showcase for the Ukrainian designers we work with, but which would also be a showcase for our anchor brand, Comme des Garçons."

How important is the design concept for you?

"It is everything. Good design is good communication, and I believe that if you can give a sense of theater relevant to your collections, then you will create a memorable shopping experience."

How about the architecture of the building?

"Atelier 1 is based in the heart of the Vozdvizhensky Hotel in Kiev. The space, which is triple-height, was actually the site of a sixteenth-century apothecary's garden. The spirituality and resonance of this was something we wanted to capture within the shop... We sell Comme des Garçons per-fumes as well as Catherine Memmi's bath and body collections; these products, which perfume the store, became our modern herb garden.

Above left
An antique case casually placed at the end of a rail is used to help create the overall theme of the store. The graphic of the gentleman printed in subdued colors helps to define the menswear floor.

Above right
Fixed rails are used to show edited collections of the store's fashion offerings. The hand-blown glass lampshades are used throughout the store and are reminscent of garden cloches.

We took the English garden shed as a working motif, and the design was initially informed by the order through chaos that is prevalent in that kind of environment. We used raw-edged metal, polished and untreated cement, and glass to contemporize the story. We wanted a large walk-in area that could be multifunctional: a space for people just to gather, sit, drink, and relax. Once this area was designed, it was clear that the impact had to be the main triple-height wall. The collections were integrated around the outer edges, with only one rail actually on the wall."

How important is it to consider the product while designing and planning the store?

"Without a clear understanding of your product you have no store. We could have introduced any brands, but knew that only one, Comme des Garçons, would share our views on presentation and merchandising. With this in mind, we threw convention out the window and allowed creativity to flourish."

How important is the in-store visual merchandising to you?

"Visual merchandising is vital. It is the lifeblood of any store and we rely on it to illustrate to our customer our message for the brand on which we are focusing."

You have used many "found" objects to accessorize your store. How did you go about sourcing them? Did you have a specific look in mind beforehand?

"The majority of the found objects have come from the U.K. We scoured our homes and any antique shops we could find to assemble a very specific look. It was also a complete process of revision for us, because objects such as two kitchen tables discarded in a cellar at home were repainted and distressed to the color scheme of the shop. The metal chairs have already had a good life living outdoors and can now be utilized inside, complete with rust and lichen attached."

The use of photography is evident in the store. How did you decide which image to use?

"We knew that to inform the space a large image was needed, and this became the main focus wall. To differentiate the men's floor, we

photographed our own images and made this into a statement for the floor."

How often do you re-merchandise your store?

"Re-merchandising for us is constant, but what differentiates us is that we focus on one brand or element per month. This means that for each month we dedicate the main selling space, the window, and all of our public relations and customer focus entirely [to] this one specific brand. Within that there will still be adjacencies. We will choose which designer collection to show and then choose which elements of perfume to work with and which collection of accessories. This allows us to have almost 12 separate stories per year. The press enjoys the variety, as do our customers. We also have salon shows for our customers every month, again focused on the selection for that month."

Above
Semi-industrial architectural features, including cement floors and exposed brickwork, act as a strong backdrop for the clothing.

Fixtures

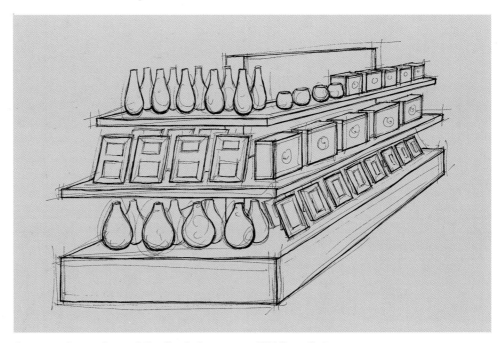

Once you have planned the final store layout, it is time to select the fixtures that will be needed to house and present the merchandise. The use of the correct fixture is paramount in producing sales. Selecting the correct fixtures may at first seem daunting. Choosing a structure that holds the correct number of products and shows them to best advantage is never easy. There are two universal styles of fixture that most retailers will use: mid-floor and linear. They can be used in conjunction with each other and both come in various forms.

Mid-floor fixtures

A mid-floor fixture is freestanding and can be used not only to carry merchandise but also to steer customers through the store. They can be shopped from all angles, making them a useful merchandising commodity. Ideally they should not be so high that they obscure other areas of the store. Their proportion should also suit the products they are housing; small items may get lost and look insignificant on a large fixture. There are many different types of mid-floor fixtures, ranging from purpose-built gondolas to tables and found items, some of which are more suited to displaying fashion and some to housewares, while many can be used for either purpose.

Above
This three-shelf gondola is typically used to display houseware items. Larger items are ideally placed at the bottom and smaller ones at the top to achieve visual balance. The center of the top shelf can be used for signage.

Opposite
Habitat uses two sizes of mid-floor fixture, each is a contemporary version of a gondola that has been specifically designed to display housewares in its Regent Street flagship store in London. The taller fixtures are used to hold larger quantities of stock. The lower fixtures are used to display china that can best be appreciated by the customer looking down on the pattern. This type of display also gives the impression of how the china would look when used on a table.

Gondola Uses

Housewares:
candles, vases

Food:
pre-packaged items

Special occasions:
Valentine's Day gifts, Christmas

Gondolas

A gondola fixture is most commonly used in home and food stores. Gondolas can be any size, but most are rectangular and have shelves on all four sides. The ends are referred to as gondola ends or endcaps. The shelves are often adjustable, making them flexible and able to house most product categories. Gondolas can be repositioned on the shop floor, provided they are easy to move. Many have lighting built into them and will require an electrical socket to be positioned nearby, ideally under the unit. Themes and stories (see pages 54–60) can easily be presented using gondola fixtures. It is important never to use too many different products; a clearly defined offer will have more impact. It is wise to remember that a gondola fixture should be filled to its capacity—it is a selling tool, not a display instrument. On many occasions retailers stock the lower shelves with smaller items that are difficult to make a strong selling point with, or create a grouping of products on the top shelf that may be easily tampered with. Larger items should always be placed at the bottom of the gondola, with smaller items at the top. The lowest shelf should be at least 1 ft (30 cm) off the ground; customers should not be expected to stoop to shop. Many gondolas have slots at the top where signage can be placed. The signage should just simply state what the gondola is carrying.

Above
A mix of secure, glass-topped floor fixtures is used to display Colette's range of valuable gadgets and high-tech equipment in the Paris store.

Tables

Tables used as merchandise fixtures can be purchased or custom-made. They are an interesting way of breaking up a floor and are easily browsed. It can be a good idea to place a lower, smaller table partially underneath a higher one, creating two height levels that will give more impact than one. Customers often feel comfortable shopping from a table because it is an object that will be familiar to them in their homes. Folded garments or items of homeware suit tables best. Clothing items should not be stacked too high; one of each size will generally suffice. A half-mannequin or bust form can be used to show the item of clothing displayed on the table. Housewares may be piled higher. It should be remembered that tables are very high-maintenance and they will need constant attention to keep them presentable.

Above
Murano glassmaker Carlo Moretti displays his wares in minimally merchandised displays on tables, creating a gallery effect that shows the quality and design of the glass to its best advantage.

Below
Folded shirts on two tables, one higher than the other, in the men's formalwear department in Selfridges, London, help lead the customer toward the back wall fixture.

Furniture Uses

Housewares:
folded items such as bedlinen, china

Hanging items:
capsule collections of clothing can be
hung in wardrobes

For smaller cabinets:
jewelry

Found Object Uses

Flat surfaces:
an antique table can be used to
display traditional china

Plinths:
can be used to display vases or
pieces of sculpture

Trunks:
can be used to display blankets,
bedlinens, cushions, or boxed gifts

Baskets:
can be used to contain scarves,
umbrellas, or small items for the home

Glass mid-floor fixtures will
always appear lighter than
solid wooden ones.

Furniture

Cabinets and cupboards are often used to present merchandise. They can be used to create theater while also functioning as a useful selling fixture. Jeans, for example, can be neatly folded and placed on the shelves of a cabinet, as can housewares. A cabinet can also be chosen to co-ordinate with the merchandise: china could be placed in a glass-fronted display cabinet while a capsule

collection of clothing could be hung in an open wardrobe. It is wise to remember that a cabinet may have an unattractive back that is best hidden by the back of another of the same size. Care should be taken to light the merchandise inside a cupboard because it is enclosed. It can be tricky to do, so it is sensible to ensure that there are sufficient overhead spotlights to focus on the product, or even to add undershelf lighting.

Above
These simple freestanding fixtures in Dover Street Market, London, are not used to show products but to create an exhibition of macabre items. They encourage customers to pause in the shop and then hopefully look at the merchandise around them.

Below
Found objects including antique chairs, cabinets, and chandeliers work alongside contemporary clothing and mannequins to create the eccentric style of London's Dover Street Market.

Found objects

Trunks, crates, and plinths are just a few found objects that can be used to present merchandise. They may have nothing in common with the majority of the other fixtures but can often change the pace and appearance of parts of the store if utilized well, such as antique pieces used alongside contemporary fixtures to provide contrast. They can also be cost-effective and may be recycled,

too. It is important that found objects are there to serve a purpose; a personal favorite from home is not acceptable unless it can help sell. A shrewd retailer will also mark these items up and sell them, thus providing the opportunity to replace them with other original pieces.

Above

These traditional glass display cabinets in Baccarat's showroom in Paris take on a modern twist, with lighting breaking through the glass ceiling from a huge suspended boulder of crystal, demonstrating the quirky style of the designer, Philippe Starck.

Housing expensive crystal, the cabinets are enclosed and secure, but allow the customer a 360-degree view.

Vendor fixtures

A vendor fixture is given by the supplier to the retailer to house and display the vendor's branded products. These fixtures can be either permanent or temporary. The advantage of using a vendor fixture is that it will not cost the retailer anything, and will be designed to carry that specific product and in the correct quantities, adding brand recognition for the customers. On many occasions retailers will have no choice but to use them if they wish to carry the brand. Such fixtures can, however, be a hindrance. Although they may enforce the brand name, they may not fit in with the store appearance. A branded fixture is, however, best used to its full advantage and not hidden away; hiding or disguising fixtures in dark corners will not fool the customer and will only alienate the vendor.

Branded shop fixtures

Like a vendor fixture, a branded shop fixture will enforce the brand image and be designed to complement the products. Sometimes known as shops-within-shops, or concessions, the product is supplied by the brand and not bought by the host store. Carefully selected by the host store and with regard to the correct product adjacencies on the floor, these shops-within-shops can enhance the overall floor layout and help to change the pace of and improve customer circulation, maintaining the interest of customers as they work their way from shop to shop. Many retailers will use them as an anchor for the whole floor; a prestigious brand will certainly grab shoppers' attention if placed in a prominent position. Seasonally, a branded shop fit can change dramatically; a designer may insist that the store changes its appearance to suit the collection by adding different graphics and signage and by re-merchandising the area.

Concept shop fits

Many retailers today that specialize in one specific product or style of merchandise have pushed the boundaries when designing their stores. Most of these retail environments have become concept stores that rely heavily on the following of their loyal customers. A concept store should be designed with the product in mind, with custom features, and strong branding and graphics.

Above

Offspring's concession within a department store features product-specific fittings, including wall fixtures designed to hold individual shoes, low mid-floor fixtures that are easy to shop from, and seating for customers trying on shoes. In-store concessions will have their own loyal fans. Offspring customers visiting the shop-within-a-shop might then be tempted to purchase from another concession within the store.

Above
Supreme is a skateboarding store
in Los Angeles, with a loyal customer
following. Their store includes a half-
pike to test the skateboards, but
which also undoubtedly creates a
dynamic atmosphere.

Specialist fixtures

Certain products will only lend themselves to specialist fixtures. Fresh produce that needs to be refrigerated will often need a specifically designed fixture. Although an open-fronted chilled fixture may not be aesthetically pleasing, it is still essential that it performs well, and products can still be arranged in a creative display. Chiller and freezer cabinets should also be designed so that they can hold large quantities; the owner of a sandwich shop will expect to sell a lot of stock over lunchtime, so having to restock a cabinet constantly would be senseless.

Ribbons, beads, and fresh flowers, to name a few, will more often than not need some considerable thought as to how they are best displayed. Beads, for example, because of their size, will need to be positioned close to eye level so that they may be viewed more comfortably. Ribbons may need to be

measured and cut by the salesperson and should be easily accessible for this purpose. Fresh flowers obviously require water; buckets may be disguised inside purpose-built shelving or display units.

Any product category can be merchandised effectively if consideration is given not only to the product but also to the customer.

Above left
A natural-wood shop design for paper products creates a tactile experience in this Prints store in Singapore. Three types of display are used: cards are placed upright; writing paper is set on angled shelves; and gift boxes are stacked onto wall fixtures.

Below left
Specifically designed to display the rolls of ribbon, these fixtures as used by VV Rouleaux in London are accessible and easy to maintain with their curved shelves.

Above right
Custom-made clear Perspex wall brackets have been designed to hold the latest mobile phones in this O2 store in Munich. The need for and design of such fixtures require investment and should be planned the same time as the store architecture.

Above
This innovative method of displaying wine, as used in Selfridges, Manchester, creates a contemporary backdrop to the futuristic bar. Each bottle is tilted at an angle so that the customer can see the label.

Below
The futuristic design of this optician, l.a.Eyeworks in Los Angeles, gives the impression of cleanliness amid a technologically advanced environment. Atmospheric lighting, clean lines, and mirror-backed glass shelves are used to promote the latest eyewear, while the mirrors are also effective as a practical tool for customers trying on the glasses.

Capacity Rail Uses

High-density stock

All types of clothing where showing range of sizes or suits

Hanging rails

Rails designed to hold garments come in many sizes and shapes. They can be purchased from wholesalers or made to order. There are two basic styles that can be used: capacity and single-bar rails.

Capacity rails

A capacity rail, as the name implies, is a capacity fixture designed to show many options of garments and carry a large amount of stock for a high product turnover. They are usually made from metal and have several adjustable arms that hold the hangers in position; they can be shopped either from two sides, known as a two-way, or four, known as a four-way, or they can be hung on a wall as part of a wall fixture (see above). It is worth thinking about the height at which the arms are set—if they are too high they may be harder to shop from. The products hang facing the customer; smaller sizes should be placed at the front and larger ones at the back. They are best utilized to show just one style of garment in many sizes, or items that together make up an outfit, like a jacket and pants. Since they are easy to replenish, large chain retailers often favor them. They are also easy to maneuver and can be repositioned to suit the products.

Above
Here polo shirts are displayed on four-way capacity rails at Topman in London. Each prong holds one style in several sizes. Smaller sizes should be hung at the front and the largest at the back.

Single rails

Stores selling more expensive clothing often use a single running rail, no different from a conventional running clothes rail. The single straight rail is best used to show fashion collections or a trend theme. They should not be overstocked; leaving one to two finger widths of space between each hanger is ideal for the customer to remove and replace garments easily. Colors should always run from left to right along the rail, starting with the lightest. Sizes should also start with the smallest on the left progressing to the largest on the right. The hangers should all be the same style and shape, with the opening facing away from the customer; in this way the garment will be easy to remove and replace.

Circular rails

Circular single rails, positioned in the middle of the shop floor, were also fashionable during the 1970s and acted in the same way as a straight rail. Today they are frowned upon, appearing clumsy and offering no flexibility. But they can be useful for presenting one piece of discounted merchandise through its spectrum of different colors, such as T-shirts.

Single Rail Uses

One type of garment

A whole collection

Sale items

Above
Three single rails positioned against a plain wall helps create an eye-catching display area for a designer collection in Dover Street Market, London.

Wall fixtures

Slatwall and Gridwall Uses

Any fashion items

Housewares

Fixed Rail Uses

Hanging clothing items

Not only can a well-merchandised wall produce great sales, but it can also be used as a backdrop for a specific product area. Some systems are more flexible than others. Many retailers favor an arrangement that can offer as many options as possible. Smaller boutiques often incorporate the linear fixtures into the store design and so may not be so concerned about being able to change the configurations.

Slatwall and gridwall systems

Large chains often use a slatwall or gridwall system because of the flexibility each can offer. They are generally designed and used to show high-turnover products because they can be replenished easily. Best used for showing fashion garments, they can also support shelves for housewares or to support a display above eye level. There are various components that can be purchased and used with these systems, such as brackets, rails, and shelves. There are many options for brackets available for all types of fashion items. The most common is the waterfall bracket that holds more than one item and which is available either as a horizontal or angled-down version. The bar itself features spacing nodules which hangers can sit in or against. A straight arm without spacing nodules will hold more merchandise because the hangers will not be spaced. Both are available as round, square, or rectangular. Many retailers build up a kit that they draw from when required.

A slatwall is made up of panels of wood that are painted or laminated and fixed directly onto the wall. The components simply slot into the gaps between the strips. A gridwall consists of a sturdy wire grid that also fixes directly to the wall, and the bracket clips onto it. Neither system is particularly aesthetic when stripped of its merchandise. It is always advisable to ensure that the brackets are placed close enough together so that when the product is hanging from them, the system is hidden. Ideally a slatwall or gridwall system should be painted the same color as the wall, enabling it to blend in with, and not overshadow, the product.

Fixed rails

A fixed sturdy rail that carries fashion garments will always look smarter than a rail supported by a slatwall or gridwall system. However, remember that they will not offer the same flexibility. A strong metal or wooden rail is often supported by wall brackets at each end of the pole. It is imperative that not only is the pole strong enough to take the weight of the garments but that the brackets are, too; winter clothing in particular can be heavy.

Above
Many components are used in this
Miss Sixty wall layout in Barcelona:
shelves, hanging rails, and innovative
wall panels used to display jeans.

Fixed shelves

As with a fixed rail, a shelf securely attached to a wall offers no flexibility but may be visually pleasing. A shelf may be attached using brackets that are used as a design feature, or by an invisible bracket that is screwed to the wall with the shelf casing slid over it, concealing the hardware. Walls with natural alcoves suit shelving; planned carefully they can create interesting merchandise areas. Shelves can be constructed from various materials, including wood, metal, glass, and acrylic. Consideration of the product should be taken into account when introducing shelves to a store. If they are to carry weighty items, a glass shelf may not be appropriate as it may break. Acrylic shelves are prone to scratching and may warp if overstocked. Wooden shelves are best laminated or lacquered; hand-painted glossy paints or emulsions will scratch easily.

Lighting shelves can be difficult; the deeper the shelf, the more shadow it will cast on the shelf below it. Ceiling spotlights can be aimed at the shelved wall; however, the lower the shelves, the less light they are likely to get. An alternative is undershelf lighting, which can be fixed to wooden or metal shelves.

Fixed Shelf Uses

Housewares

Fashion items

Opposite
Stylish fixed shelving throughout the Alexander McQueen store in New York is used to exhibit women's accessories in this high-end fashion store. Concealed lighting is incorporated into the underside of the shelves.

Above
These fixed alcove shelves in Miss Sixty's Barcelona store have been created to house items of folded clothing. Clever use of low-voltage halogen lighting highlights the product in what could be a dark box.

Product handling

There are numerous ways to merchandise both mid-floor and wall fixtures, some of which are more suited to walls than mid-floor fixtures, or vice versa. Gaining a knowledge of these basic principles will aid any newcomer to visual merchandising.

Color blocking

Using the color of the product to create visual impact is the simplest and most fundamental way of presenting any type of merchandise. From T-shirts and towels to cans of paint and crockery, each product category can create a functional yet bold display. The skill of color blocking is not difficult to master. This style of product handling is low-maintenance and easy to replenish. It is often favored by large superstores and chain stores and can be applied to both wall and mid-floor fixtures.

Horizontal merchandising

This style of merchandising is best suited to wall fixtures. Merchandise is hung or shelved in horizontal rows. Each shelf or row of the fixture may be arranged by color or by the same style of product item, such as a row of floral T-shirts or a series of square vases. Ideally, one product per row is better than several. This style of presentation is more functional and easy to replenish. It is worth noting that products placed at either the top or the bottom of the fixture will not attract the same attention as those placed at eye level.

Above
Knitwear in neutral tones is displayed from the top to the foot of these shelves in Uniqlo's store in Tokyo. Smaller sizes should be placed at the top and larger at the bottom. Top shelves that shoppers cannot reach can hold extra stock.

Below
Ladies' knitwear has been color blocked in this Marks & Spencer store, creating an eye-catching, aesthetic display that is easy to shop from.

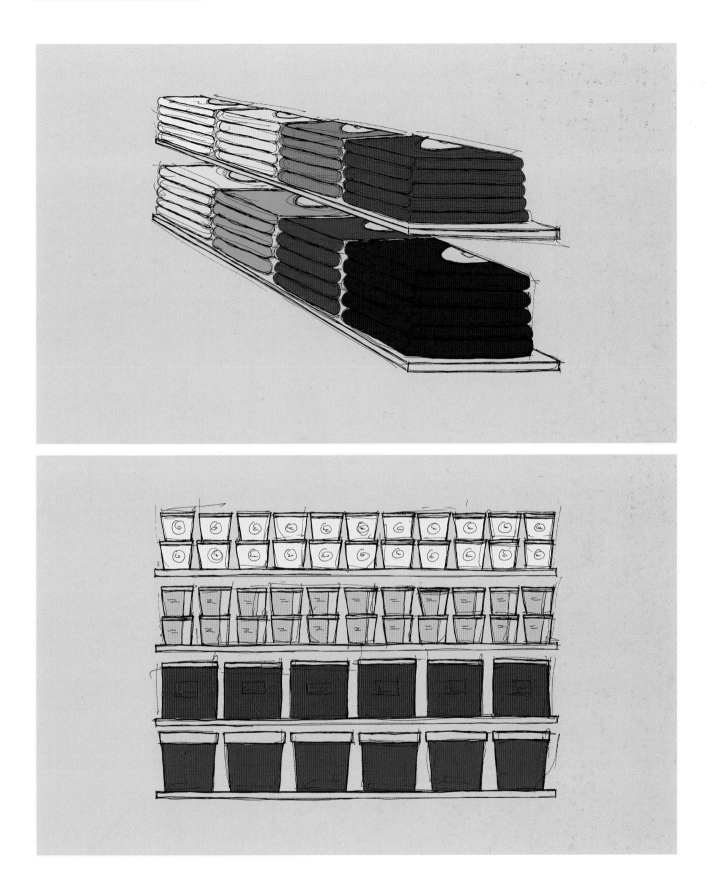

Above
Color blocking is one of the simplest
and most effective ways to display
product, by grouping items by color.
It is easy to maintain, replenish, and
shop from, and can be applied to both
fashion and housewares.

Below
Horizontal merchandising is a
simple term for products being
shelved or hung horizontally from
left to right. Larger items should
be placed at the bottom and smaller
at the top. It is important that
shelves or rails are positioned
as close to each other as possible
so that there are no gaps that could
weaken the impact.

Vertical merchandising

As with horizontal merchandising, this format uses lines of products, but this time running from top to bottom of the wall. It can be used to show the different product options available and can be merchandised by color. As with the horizontal format, this style is easy to replenish and functional.

Product blocking

This style of merchandising is best used for volume merchandise. Generally, a fixture or wall is stocked with just one product category or range. Product blocking shows authority and creates impact. The use of this style of merchandising is logical for the customer because it shows the colors and sizes clearly. Product-blocked fixtures are low-maintenance and easy to replenish.

Symmetrical merchandising

As the name suggests, symmetrical merchandising is a style of presenting the product to create a mirrored effect. This method is only suited to wall fixtures. The product is presented in the same way on each side, with an imaginary line running vertically through the middle. Symmetrical merchandising will require more wall space than would be necessary to show a complete product range, purely because the same product is duplicated.

Above
Vertical merchandising is the display of product from left to right and top to bottom and, again, is suitable for clothing or homeware. It is also easy to replenish and shop.

Above

Product blocking is used here in a layout for men's T-shirts and shorts. Brackets have been used to show face-out items, and rods used for products hung in profile. This type of display is efficient for fast-turnover products, especially for fashion items.

Below

Using a wall fixture with its shelving, brackets and rods, products are displayed symmetrically. This type of display is easy to create and is pleasing to the eye. The bust form can be used to draw attention to the display or highlight an item of clothing.

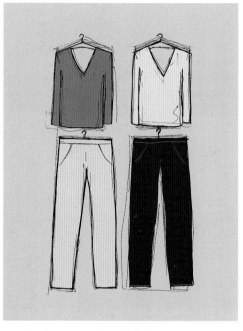

Checkered merchandising

Checkered merchandising is effective and easy to execute on wall fixtures. It relies on the use of color to create impact. Like a checkerboard, products are alternated along a length of wall. The overall effect should be balanced and symmetrical.

Anatomical merchandising

This style of merchandising is only suited to fashion items. The idea is to hang the garments on top of each other in the same way they would be worn: i.e. shirts under jackets. Anatomical merchandising creates complete, defined looks and can be used for mixed product types.

Above left
An effective use of wall space that relies solely on the merchandising to produce the effect, checkering uses two colors alternately to create a checkerboard pattern. This is useful for enlivening basics such as T-shirts and knitwear.

Above right
Whether on a wall or mid-floor fixture, anatomical merchandising is used to display fashion items where garments are displayed as they would be worn— such as a top displayed above pants. This type of display can be used to inspire a look or a fashion trend.

Co-ordinated merchandising

Fashion or houseware category groups benefit from using the co-ordinated merchandising technique. Collections or themes are grouped together to create a cohesive look. A jacket would be hung with a co-ordinating shirt and could be accessorised with a co-ordinated tie hung with it. A sofa could be displayed with a co-ordinated cushion, rug, and throw, placed on or around it.

This type of co-ordinated merchandising can also be applied to housewares. To create a co-ordinated look, you might put cushions, curtains, throws, and associated soft furnishing products together, depending on their style or trend; a traditional floral print could be broken up with plain knits and traditional stripes to create a French Provençal look, whereas muted grays and naturals could be highlighted with accent colors, such as bold pinks, reds, or blues, for a contemporary look

that would suit an inner-city loft. These looks are designed to give the customer inspiration and educate them on how to put products together effectively.

Displaying product collections

The alternative to co-ordinated merchandising is to show collections which demonstrate the authority of the range in-store. Instead of dispersing candles throughout the home floor, co-ordinating them with textiles and ceramics, they can all be housed together to create an authoritative selection of varying colors, sizes, styles, and prices. This will give customers a clear understanding of the range of candles on offer but leave them to make their own selection.

Above
Co-ordinated merchandising is the art of placing products together in the hope that customers will buy more than one item. The aim is to create a "look" for them. Here at Dover Street Market in London, shoes, dresses, jackets and coats are on display.

Store study: Flight 001

Flight 001 is a unique concept store specializing in travel goods and catering for the jet-setter's every need. The founders, Brad John and John Sencion, interviewed together here, both began their careers in retail and design.

Their first store in New York drew attention from both the public and the media. Now with stores across the U.S. and in Dubai, Flight 001 is gaining international recognition.

Every design detail has been considered, from the overall shell of the stores that resembles the interior of an aircraft to the linear and mid-floor fixtures and the strong graphics that reinforce the brand's identity. The diversity of the collection ranges from keyrings to suitcases, and care has been taken how best to display each item. Because of these details and the product mix, Flight 001 remains an innovative concept store.

Your store is very product-specific. Was it challenging designing a store that has to show so many different product categories?

"Yes, it has been challenging but it is something we enjoy doing. Our store design has been an evolutionary process, beginning with the first prototype where we made some design decisions about rounding the corners in the space but designed only one fixture: the ticket-counter register. Before opening our first store we didn't know the characteristics and dimensions of all our products, so by the time we opened the next store two years later, we knew that we needed to create adjustable shelves for the side walls. In the third store we made an attempt to figure out the center-floor fixtures, but it wasn't until the fourth store that we perfected them. We have now addressed all our product categories and are currently working on smaller display fixtures for all these products."

Was the overall store design important?

"The overall design of the store was extremely important. When we opened our first store in 1999, 'design' per se was a dormant faculty for the general public. It was only after the turn of the century (and millennium) that the idea of 'design' as a concept was awakened and came alive. Back in 1999 we felt it was a differentiating decision not just to throw paint on the walls and open a store. At the time our attention to a store design concept made us different. Design was an option then, but today design is not an option when opening a successful store—it's a must."

How did you decide on the complete look for the first flagship store?

"Our travel concept has always made decisions easy and entertaining for us because it is so focused and directed. We use travel as a

Above left
Flight 001's concept travel stores are designed to resemble the interior of an aircraft fuselage. Because the store is open-fronted and the customer can look straight in, it is important that the interior is always merchandised to a high standard.

Above right
For a store that is solely reliant on the travel customer, luggage is a key product category. A light-box with a retro graphic of a case is placed dead center on the back wall, thus pulling the customers through to the luggage area at the rear of the shop.

metaphor when making design, brand, and 'terminology' (language) decisions, so an international airplane lounge was an obvious inspirational choice for our store prototype."

Has each of the fixtures been specifically designed with the product in mind?

"Absolutely. We have several fixture options based on our broad product assortment. We have a general area on the side walls consisting of adjustable shelves. These shelves include back-stock storage bins at the very bottom. Center-aisle showcases are used for more expensive, smaller items. We have an essentials peg wall used to merchandise smaller, unattractive products that we repackage, and in the back of the stores we have the same adjustable shelving without storage bins that we use for luggage and large travel bags."

How do you decide the overall layout of the store's products?

"We have a center runway aisle that makes it easy for customers to move from the front to the back of the stores. When we originally put the store layout on paper, we used zones to identify certain areas based on the departments we thought would be important, as well as the product adjacencies.

The cash desk acts as an anchor to the store and is designed not to overshadow any of the fixtures or products. Even the front of the cabinet has been glazed to house expensive items such as watches. A low table opposite does not crowd the space for waiting customers, and the wall behind it has not been heavily merchandised so that the area is free for customers at the cash register."

Are the product adjacencies important in driving sales?

"Yes. We think of adjacencies as 'suggestive selling.' So, if you are buying personal-care items, you might consider placing a toiletry bag to carry all these products right next to it."

Do you use any vendor fixtures? If so, do they work with your brand aesthetically and practically?

"It is always a challenge to use vendor fixtures because they often don't have the same design aesthetic we have within our store.

We do use vendor fixtures when they are functional and in line with our brand."

How important is signage to your stores?

"Signage is our dialogue in courting our customers, so it is very important. The challenge is making signage unobtrusive but meaningful.

The true meaning of concept is an idea, a thought, or a notion. With this in mind it is always worth considering why a store may be considered a 'concept' store. Having twice as much merchandise in a larger space does not qualify, nor does designing an elaborate shop arrangement to carry a collection already available in other stores. A true and successful concept store like Flight 001 has an interesting product mix, innovative store design, and a retail ethos that helps support the brand and sustain customer interest."

Above
The design of fixtures to work with the product is very apparent in the Chicago store. Enclosed glass display cases are used for small, high-value items, while adjustable open shelves carry the bulk of the merchandise. Drawers resembling overhead lockers are used for storage.

Below
The merchandising of the shelves is carefully conceived, with color blocking used for bags on shelves on the left-hand side. The placement of a lower fixture adjacent to or opposite a higher one gives the impression of space and does not crowd the entrance to the shop, or block the smaller items in the shelves behind it.

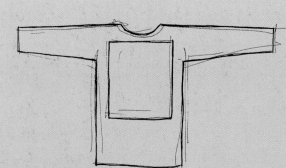

Step 1
Lay the garment on a flat, clean surface. Ensure that the item has no creases. At this stage, tissue paper may be placed on the garment. Place the folding board on top of the tissue or directly onto the garment.

Step 2
Fold the left sleeve onto the board and over onto the right arm.

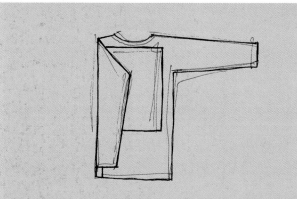

Step 3
Then fold the arm down vertically so that the back of the sleeve is facing up.

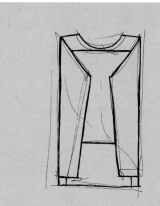

Step 4
Repeat with the right sleeve.

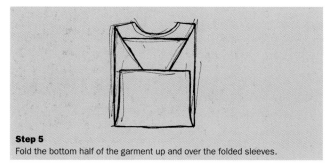

Step 5
Fold the bottom half of the garment up and over the folded sleeves.

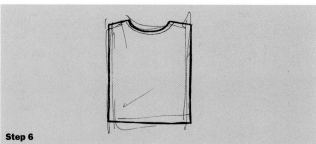

Step 6
Turn the board and garment over and slide the folding board out.

Prepping fashion items

Depending on whether a retailer uses wall fixtures or mid-floor fixtures, all product items, whether fashion, housewares or perishable goods, will still need to be presented correctly. This is known as "prepping."

Hanging garments should be unpacked and "prepped"—and ideally should follow the useful guidelines opposite.

Folding boards

A folding board is a useful tool that will enable anyone who is folding clothes to make certain that all the folded items will be the same size. They are, however, only useful for folding knitwear, T-shirts, and shirts. They are usually made from either wood or Perspex, and can be made to suit the size of specific shelves.

Above
Folding boards create great results for folding tops, such as T-shirts.

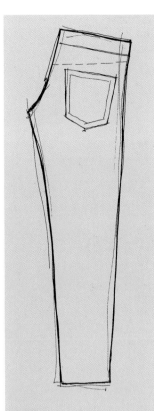

Step 1
Fold the pants (without folding board) into themselves so that the back pockets are both visible. Lay the folded garment on a clean surface. Ensure that the item has no creases.

Step 2
Fold in the "seat" of the pants so that the outstretched garment appears straight.

Step 3
Take the end of the leg and bring it up to just below the back pocket.

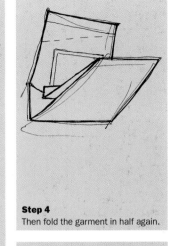

Step 4
Then fold the garment in half again.

Step 5
If the item has a label on the back pocket, this should be clearly visible.

Erin Thompson, head of visual merchandising for Selfridges, London, employs strict rules that are adhered to across the fashion floors that she oversees. Her tips are:

Items should be ironed or steamed.

- - - - - - - - - - - - - - - - - - - -

Price tags should be attached to the label, or where least likely to mark the garment, and should be tucked into the garment so that they are not visible.

- - - - - - - - - - - - - - - - - - - -

Alarm tags should be placed through a seam in the garment.

- - - - - - - - - - - - - - - - - - - -

Hangers should be hung on the rail and all facing the same way.

- - - - - - - - - - - - - - - - - - - -

All merchandise should be grouped in size order, starting with the smallest items on top.

- - - - - - - - - - - - - - - - - - - -

Merchandise should be grouped by color categories.

- - - - - - - - - - - - - - - - - - - -

Jackets and tops should be shown in front of pants.

- - - - - - - - - - - - - - - - - - - -

Keep products grouped together.

- - - - - - - - - - - - - - - - - - - -

Make sure that a maximum of six to eight items are stacked together.

- - - - - - - - - - - - - - - - - - - -

Ensure that all of the stacks of folded product on a shelf unit are all the same height.

- - - - - - - - - - - - - - - - - - - -

Ensure all of the shelves are clean and dust-free.

- - - - - - - - - - - - - - - - - - - -

A folding board should be used for tops.

Above
Pants are best folded using the above technique, for which folding boards are not used.

Housewares will also need prepping. Bear the following guidelines in mind:

All products should be cleaned.

Sticky price labels should be placed on the bottom of each item.

Clear Perspex sheets should be placed in between stacked merchandise to help stabilize the products.

Product should be grouped in color categories.

Items should not be stacked so high that they are difficult to buy.

Non-fashion merchandising

Merchandising housewares or solid products differs from merchandising apparel, yet many similar techniques can be applied. If the product being displayed is to be taken directly to the cash desk by the customer, the general rule is to ensure that the collection appears authoritative and that there are sufficient amounts available; a customer purchasing plates may require only one or a whole set. Exclusive, expensive items should not be duplicated or their perceived value will be diminished. Understanding the correct quantities to show depends on the price and the expected turnover. Volume products can, however, be stacked high and will look appealing, especially during sale times.

Food items can also benefit from visual merchandising theories and practices. Many types of fruit and vegetables can benefit from color blocking. Yellow, green, and red peppers, for instance, look visually stronger when grouped together by their color. By piling their produce high, market stall-holders attract customers by demonstrating their product authority. The high turnover of the

merchandise would not suit a minimal presentation, which may send a mixed message to consumers, telling them that the produce is highly priced because of the minimal presentation. Expensive caviars and fine wines, on the other hand, would clearly benefit from a simpler presentation; the customer on this occasion would want to be assured that these items are rare and not available to the mass market.

Above
Dark, low-level tables are used to show home accessory items in the Globus Food Hall in Zurich, Switzerland. They have been sparsely merchandised to give the impression of exclusivity. Overhead lighting is positioned over the tables to highlight the products.

Above
CDs at Colette in Paris create a band running along the wall at eye level and so are easy to shop for. Such a display creates an interesting focal point, drawing the customer toward the back of the store.

Below
Skateboards at Trust Nobody's, Barcelona, lend themselves to horizontal merchandising. Displayed on wall shelves, they are easy to view and select.

In-store displays and trend areas

"As a luxury retailer, it is paramount that we position like-minded and style-sharing vendors within the same space. Price points and brand cachet are essential considerations."

John Gerhardt, Creative Services Director, Holt Renfrew

In-store displays can be straightforward; nevertheless, there are a few guidelines that will help the presentation be more effective. Trend areas are an invention from the 1980s that is still popular today. Both are designed to attract customers and sales and work in a similar fashion.

In-store displays

The idea of either continuing the window scheme in-store or presenting a selection of products with their own theme has been used by the large department stores since they first opened. In-store displays are created to continue the theater and drama inside the shop. Usually they consist of products supported by props arranged so that they can be admired but not touched or dismantled and taken to the cash desk. On rare occasions they may be designed not to sell products but to inspire; a piece of art or an art installation may be unprofitable but will cause excitement and provoke opinions about the store's brand.

In-store displays should be created with the same care as window displays. The same layout and design principles apply, except that they are usually seen from all angles. Most in-store displays benefit from being raised up so that they may be viewed from across the store without obstructions. A strong wooden base or plinth will help elevate the presentation. Like a window display, the plinth may need to be covered or painted to co-ordinate with the theme. It is important that the plinth is sturdy enough to support the weight of the display; a thick wooden top is best so that it can have products or props securely screwed or nailed onto it. Electric sockets can also be incorporated into the structure. A permanently positioned in-store display plinth will also profit from having a fixed ceiling grid discreetly secured above it with an effective lighting track.

Above
The dramatic avant-garde display featuring a tree sculpture and kites acts as a backdrop for this display of eveningwear. It is positioned in the middle of the floor, taking up valuable sales-floor space, but its eye-catching impact will generate sales.

Above
Hundreds of electric guitars
suspended above mannequins
create an interesting musical theme
in Lane Crawford, Hong Kong.

Below
Another Lane Crawford display
features lacquered bamboo as part of
the Chinese New Year celebrations.

The main intention of all product displays is to sell. In-store displays should be used to pull customers into the store and get them to browse. If designed well, they should act as an inspirational guide. The most common use of an in-store display is to demonstrate to the customer which current trends and key looks are on offer in their host department. They are best positioned at the end of sight-lines and should be used as focal points (see page 116). If a display is dressed with products from the host department, it is essential that the merchandise used is not far away. It would be senseless to create an eye-catching presentation using products that cannot be easily found. Positioning the product fixtures adjacent to the display will encourage customers to spend purely because they would not have to look far to find the items they admired on the display.

In-store displays can also be used as a tool to inform the customer of other product categories available in the store. A furniture display placed at the foot of an escalator on the fashion floor of a department store can show the customer what else is available in the store, and with effective signage, can direct them to the location.

Maintaining in-store displays is, unfortunately, a task that will require time and patience. Many an exhausted customer has been found sitting on display plinths, often leaving discarded trash among the product groupings. Children are apt to climb up and swing from the props, and the merchandise, no matter how high, will be tampered with. Morning and evening checks will not be sufficient to keep the display pristine; encouraging the shop-floor sales staff to assume ownership of the displays can often help.

Above
A line of immaculately dressed mannequins elevated on a fixture and all wearing neutral colors makes an impressive in-store display at Lane Crawford, Hong Kong.

Below
New York's Barneys' renowned quirky sense of humor is demonstrated here with mannequins used not only to promote merchandise but also to add a whimsical touch to the fashion floor.

Trend areas

As with an in-store display, a trend area is designed to create interest and inspire the customer. In this case, however, more emphasis is placed on the product and not the props. A trend area basically contains topical products, either by trend or look. Trend areas are often seasonal mini-shops-within-a-shop; they work by promoting a new idea or collection of products grouped together, often with a small display to help reinforce the look.

The difference between a trend area and an in-store display is the fact that the customer is encouraged to shop from the former. A good example of a trend area would be a beach shop. Because of the seasonal implications of selling beachwear, the retailer only has a limited time to advertise the product. To give the story more impact, various other product-related categories such as sunglasses, hats, sandals, sarongs, and suntan lotions could be merchandised with the core beachwear. Mannequins dressed and accessorized in the relevant clothing could be positioned in the center of the merchandise fixtures to promote the trend area. Together, the complete collection can be given a name, and a brand can be created for the limited time that it is present on the shop floor. For the customer, a trend area helps solve many shopping requirements; a woman planning a vacation

can now be informed of the seasonal trends and can find most of her clothes and accessories in one place without having to search throughout the store.

Home and leisure stores rely on trend areas more than the consumer might imagine. Again, mostly based on seasonal activities, the retailer will often create themes out of new products and place them at the front of the store to encourage sales. An outdoor dining theme consisting of barbecues, garden furniture, and accessories could be placed at the front of a store in the summer months.

Christmas and other major festive dates all benefit from trend areas to help promote products. Christmas decorations that clearly have no fixed department for the rest of the year can either be grouped en masse in one area, or be split over several trend areas, each one with a different theme, such as contemporary decorations in the young fashion department and traditional decorations on the housewares floor. It is important to remember that trend areas can take up a lot of space. The department hosting one will need to be informed in good time; not only will it need to accommodate them on the floor, staff will also need to adjust their figures to compensate for the loss of floor space the trend area has taken.

Above
A trend area in the Limited Collection department of Marks & Spencer uses both a standing and a seated mannequin to demonstrate the look and trend, while the products are positioned adjacent to them.

Point of purchase and add-on sales

Many retailers maximize their sales potential by using point of purchase and add-on sales. Both are aimed at customers who have already purchased and are now being encouraged to buy other items.

Point of purchase

Anyone paying for a magazine in a news-agent's or paying for their fuel at a petrol station would have been targeted—on most occasions unwittingly—by point-of-purchase merchandise. The fixture that holds low-price items such as chewing gum, batteries and air fresheners are all point-of-purchase fixtures, usually supplied by the vendor. The power of point of purchase should not be underestimated; this is the last chance the retailer has of taking money from the customer. Volume sales at low prices can be instrumental in elevating the store's sales turnover.

Destination stores such as newstands will usually use point-of-purchase fixtures supplied by brands that are designed to carry only their products, such as chewing gum. The brands are often familiar to the customer and are a useful commodity. Point-of-purchase offers in department stores may not be as obvious. There the most common point-of-purchase item might be a gift voucher or economical collection of merchandise. For a major retailer, the most profitable point-of-purchase item would be for a customer to sign up for a store account card at the cash desk.

Add-on sales

An add-on sale differs from a point-of-purchase offer because it is generally driven by the sales staff. Retailers will often encourage their staff to try and persuade the customer to buy extra products that complement their main purchase, i.e. shoe polish or protectors for footwear sales, batteries with electrical sales, and additional flattering cosmetics in the beauty department. Not every customer is comfortable with this hard-sell technique, and it is sometimes wise to incorporate both add-on and point of purchase to gain the maximum transactions. Positioning add-on sales close to the main product categories allows customers to easily discover them by themselves.

Above
Placed adjacent to the cash registers where customers wait to pay, candy and small pick-up items are positioned to easily tempt them.

Above
Potato chips, cookies and healthy
snacks are deliberately placed near
the cash register to tempt customers
to pick up additional items. Many cash
desks will have shelves specifically
designed to sit at the front.

Clearance merchandise

Clearance lines can be presented in numerous ways:

Reduced goods can be pulled together and placed at the front of the store, enabling the customers to browse through them and then walk further into the non-sale items in-store.

Sale goods can be used as a magnet to draw customers to the back of the store, leading them past the non-sale items.

Individual departments can use selected fixtures to hold sale lines.

Larger stores, like department stores, have been known to dedicate a whole floor to sale goods, usually on the least profitable floor (often the one furthest away from the main entrance), especially when the sale has finished and there is remaining discounted merchandise that has to be sold.

Large chain stores often rely on completely separate discount stores branded under their name to move sale lines or overstocked products.

Clearance merchandise should not be overlooked. Sale times are extremely profitable for retailers. Most major stores will proudly present their discounted products twice a year and benefit from their competitors following suit and thus attracting customers to the area. Many stores will continue to sell items at a reduction all year round.

It is important to understand the store's philosophy and requirements when approaching markdowns. Many retailers hide their markdown offers toward the rear of the store, as if they are ashamed of them; others will proudly display them in the platinum and gold areas, hoping to generate on-the-spot sales, which can be more effective. Sometimes individual departments may have sale items when the rest of the store does not. In this case, a department can also adopt this process by placing the sale items at the front or back of the department.

Sales signage

It is worth considering how you wish to promote the reductions at sale times. Many retailers like to show the original price and the corresponding reduction next to it. Many also like to show the percentage saved in the sale for the customer. It is unwise to use all of these methods on one tag, however, as it may become confusing. Once your sale signage strategy is decided it is always best to apply the same approach throughout the whole store, so that the customer receives just one overall message.

Many shrewd retailers often add a phrase in small print on the tags, such as "up to xx per cent off" or "many items at xx per cent off." This is not illegal in many countries, but it is wise to check with local retailing regulators beforehand.

Above
Covering the windows with vinyl is an effective and powerful way of projecting Selfridges' sale message in London.

Signage and tagging

Nowadays, signage is not just limited to handwritten or printed information. Neon, plasma, and LED displays are some of the more modern innovative ways of communicating with the customer. Whichever style of signage a retailer chooses, it is important to understand that, whether the store is large or small, customers need to have explanations, directions, and information made clear to them.

Store guides and other navigational signs

Before customers have begun a shopping experience they often wish to orient themselves. A large store with many floors needs to have detailed store guides and product locations. Often, this information is posted just inside the main entrance or at an information desk so that the customer has time to study the store's layout before entering. Complicated store guides will only confuse consumers; it is advisable to keep the directions simple but informative. A scaled-down plan of each of the floors with key destination points such as elevators and escalators will best aid the customer. Highlighting entrances, fire exits, restaurants, and restrooms can also orient and reassure the shopper. A printed leaflet of the store guide can also be either handed to customers on entering or placed close to each entrance for shoppers to pick up themselves.

Above right
Twenty-first-century technology is used in the Prada store in Los Angeles to communicate with customers, informing them of current social and political stories with the aim of creating a talking point.

Above left
A simple neon light sign becomes a prop in itself in the hands of a mannequin at Lane Crawford in Hong Kong.

162

Above
Quirky but effective, Topshop's visual merchandisers in London have used original 45-rpm records to spell out the name of the vintage department.

Once inside, the customer may need extra help to navigate the store. Often, signs—commonly referred to as banners—are hung above walkways. Banners are usually screen-printed or have vinyl text applied to them. They can either be cut from foam board or wood or made from coated fabric. Free-standing signposts placed at the beginning of walkways, escalators, and elevators are an effective way of telling customers where they are and what else is available in-store.

Departmental signage will help the customer plot a course around and through the merchandise. A strong supplier brand can act as an anchor to reinforce the department's product category. Used correctly and as a focal point, a strong brand on a wall will pull the customer into the heart of the department. Wall signage is an integral part of store design and visual merchandising. When used correctly it can not only direct but also attract the customer. Plasma screens and neon are a quirky way of creating theater, yet confirming a message; they both can be used to add movement to bland wall fixtures.

Freestanding signs that are used to inform the customer of promotions, events, or prices should always be printed on card and ideally be displayed in a Perspex holder. Sign-holders can be made to any size, but one universal size is usually more effective. Where the sign may be viewed from both sides, two can be placed back to back, or the sign may be printed on both sides. Signs in Perspex holders should sit with the product and be an integral part of the presentation, not an afterthought. Customers often move free-standing signs, and an easy solution is to fit the sign-holder to flat surfaces with double-sided tape.

Above left
Signage does not always have to carry a serious message or direct the shopper. Sometimes a simple graphic is enough as in Kirna Zabête, New York, encouraging its customers to enjoy retail therapy.

Below left
Two bold arrows direct the customer around this Halfords car-maintenance, customizing and travel-solutions store. The use of color and graphics is also reminiscent of road signs, in order to relate to the motoring aspirations of its customers.

Above right
The success of this sign in Heal's store in London lies in its simplicity. The size of the lettering means that it is easily spotted across the shop, enabling customers to find the department easily and also drawing them across the floor.

Below right
Strong graphics and signage hang directly above fresh produce in a Safeway's supermarket in California, making it easy for the customer to identify their location in the store.

Checklist for tags:

Handwritten tags will look sloppy and unprofessional.

Always check for spelling mistakes.

Ensure the text is not too long.

Use a clear, simple typeface that is easy and large enough to read.

Use one size of tag.

Different-colored tags for different departments can be effective.

Perspex tag-holders will collect dust; they will need to be cleaned regularly.

Hanging signs must be secure; an air vent may cause them to sway.

Text and color

Directional in-store signs should have an identity of their own so that they do not blend in or clash with other graphics; a unique color or style will help them stand out. Text should be clear and simple to read and in a contrasting color to the background. It is worth noting that lower-case letters are easier to read than capitals.

As much as written information is critical to inform the customer, too much can confuse. A customer will not often have the time or patience to stop and read numerous lines of text. Short, punchy statements can be more effective.

Price tags

Pricing individual products can be executed in two ways. Some retailers may wish for the price to dominate the product; discount stores and sale items will definitely benefit from this technique. Large stickers or "hang tags" are placed on the items and stacked high to encourage high-turnover sales. Price stickers, although in a prominent location on the packaging, should not cover the brand name. All prices should be in the same place on each item, ideally to the left at either the top or the bottom. A table with multiples of just one product may require only a freestanding sign showing the price.

Retailers who may wish their products to appear more exclusive will benefit from placing price stickers either on the back or bottom of the merchandise. A small, boxed item can easily be picked up and examined for the price; placing the sticker out of sight means the customer has to engage with the product. However, larger or fragile items such as vases are best priced at the back toward the bottom; it is unwise and risky to suggest that the customer handles expensive items.

Garments should have their price tags securely attached, either with a safety pin or by using a kimble gun, which forces a small plastic tag through the fabric with a thin needle. Care should always be taken to ensure that the needle does not destroy or mark the garment. The seam or label is the most appropriate place for the tag to be attached. Retailing regulations vary in each country: some require that the price is visible on the garment; others are happy for the price to be positioned discreetly inside. It is always worth researching the local trading laws before pricing products.

Above left
At Marks & Spencers, a tag clearly designed to show price and size is attached with a kimble gun to the inside of the garment, but is still visible to the customer.

Above middle
The store guide for a department store needs to be simple and easy to read because of the amount of information that it has to carry, given that such stores will have many floors to describe. Peter Jones in London is a good example, as shown here.

Above right
On arriving at the foot of the escalator on the ground floor of Peter Jones in London, customers learn more detail of what they will find on the floor. The large "G" and fashion graphic add instant information as customers descend, with the detail listed beneath.

Printed graphics

The use of printed images will free a lot of time for a visual merchandiser. Hanging a printed banner with a picture or design on it where a product display is usually housed—or even behind a collection of mannequins—to form a backdrop will create an instant focal point. A major benefit of a printed graphic is that text can easily be added to it, so that not only will customers be aware of the image, they may also be informed by the message.

A graphic refers to a printed image that can be either a photograph, drawing, or a piece of artwork incorporating an image and text. Many graphics that appear either in store windows or in-store are connected to a brand's advertising campaign (the brand being that of the store or of the individual designer placed in a store, for example) and are often supplied in a large format that can be incorporated with the brand's shop fit. Seasonally they are removed and updated. Modern graphics are usually digitally printed at high resolution by photographic techni-cians. The cost of printing large banners digitally is minimal compared to the old screen-printing methods. Images can be any size and in full color, black-and-white, or sepia. Printed graphics, when used correctly, can change the appearance of a department or shop dramatically. They are easy to use and easy to store. Adding text to graphics

will also send a message as well as look appealing.

There are many reasons why retailers rely so heavily on graphics in-store and in windows. The major rationale is cost. During the 1980s, the cost of producing in-store displays to the same standard and quality as the windows escalated, sometimes way over the set budgets. A simple solution was to use printed backdrops to create the same drama as a display. Often they never matched the more traditional methods. Today, however, they are a much-appreciated tool that is often used with the more conventional techniques of visual merchandising.

Above
Large-scale graphics give the appearance that they have fallen at Lane Crawford, Hong Kong. The result is an interesting display with unusual angles created on the store floor.

Below
A simple collection of photographs showing Neil Barrett's menswear collection is attached to the wall to highlight the clothing in front, at the Lane Crawford store.

Above
An installation for Costume National in the atrium of Lane Crawford, Hong Kong. It was loosely based on its showroom and only lasted one month.

Below
Universally, cosmetic counters utilize backlit transparencies to promote their brand and product range, as shown here in a department store in Tokyo.

Backlit transparencies

Most perfumery counters around the world prove how effective backlit transparencies can be. Simply put, the box that houses the transparency consists of a light-box with four sides and a row of fluorescent lamps at the back. A Perspex or glass sheet at the front supports the transparency. More often than not, the frame supporting the Perspex or glass will unclip, making it easy for the image to be replaced. The image is produced as a transparency by a photographer and, like the digital graphic, can come in various sizes. Often brands will supply their own transparencies.

Backlit transparencies are cost-effective and very low-maintenance. Once the unit is fixed to a wall or fixture, it needs little attention. They are a great tool to brighten up a dull corner of a store as well as send an important message to the consumer.

Above
A large backlit transparency acts as a focal point to attract customers at Benetton, Moscow.

Lighting

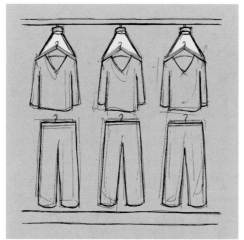

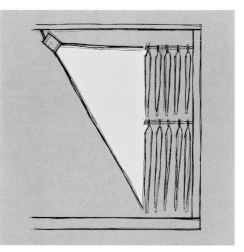

Lighting should never be an afterthought. The following should always be considered when creating a display:

Does the display lend itself to lighting?

Is the display in an area accessible to electric sockets or a lighting track?

How will the display be lit?

What fittings are required to light it?

Lighting plays an integral part in any retail environment, whether it is used for highlighting an in-store focal point or simply to flood the fixtures with enough light so that the customers can easily find what they are looking for (see Lighting chart on page 202). On no account will lighting be the most economical item in the visual merchandiser's budget; good-quality, effective light fixtures can be expensive.

Unfortunately, retailers do not always utilize lighting rigs to their full extent. Many still place all of their efforts into dressing the display, yet fail to make it stand out with the use of good lighting. Often the most exciting visual areas in a store are hidden in the shadows.

A track system with adjustable lights offers the most flexibility for in-store displays and gives the visual merchandiser the opportunity to use several different lamp fittings, each of which will perform a different role within the display. Spots will highlight an individual piece of merchandise, while floods will give an ambient light to the whole.

The wattage and beam width of a lamp can be baffling to a novice. The actual lamp fitting is useless without the correct lamp. Many light fixtures can house a variety of lamps, but not all of them will be universally effective. The size of the beam width you require usually depends on the size of the grouping it is expected to highlight. A small product item such as jewelry, for example, will only require a three-degree beam width; anything wider will illuminate the surrounding area. Shop floors are often lit with fluorescent strip lighting which, when used properly, gives an overall ambient light that is effective and efficient.

Above left
When lighting a wall, lights should be adjusted so that the beams are focused on the clothes and not on empty adjacent walls, floor, or ceiling. The lamps should always face the wall and should not be directed into the shop, blinding the customers.

Above right
The correct-sized beam width should be used: anything too small will highlight just one section of a garment; anything too wide will spill over the presentation.

Above

Fluorescent strip lighting used in an unconventional way creates an impressive focal point at the entrance into the men's designer section.

Below

Paying attention to the lighting of products and props can make the difference between a successful display and one that does not work.

Ambience

Conventional visual merchandising may not always be enough to get the overall ambience of the store right. Retailers worldwide strive to offer their customers experiences that are not just merchandise-led. Interaction from a DJ or the tasting of food are just two of the experiences that today's customer now expects.

Music

The visual merchandiser's role often might not stop at laying out the shop floor and ensuring that the store is presentable and promoting the brand image. Today, it is likely that visual merchandisers will also be called upon to look at the overall level of the store's ambience and atmosphere. They may be asked to decide if music should be played while the customers shop, and if so, what they should be listening to.

Music undoubtedly will add ambience; however, it is wise to consider which music suits the style of merchandise and the customer. A loud din of contemporary music may be offputting to an older woman shopping

for curtains while it might inspire a younger audience browsing in a jeans shop. It may also be sensible to check that the lyrics are not offensive.

Aromas and scents

Aromas and scents will stimulate the senses of shoppers—provided that the customer likes the smell. Atmospheric aromas can also be introduced to an area that warrants them and can help to promote a product. Scented candles displayed in an aromatic environment will boost sales.

Some aromas are linked to their product category, particularly if that is an item of food, but it is always best to ensure that items are fresh. Nasty smells will, of course, be offputting; disguising them will only act as a short-term solution. The aroma of freshly baked bread in a bakery will entice the customer to spend, yet the smell of stale fish in a fish seller's shop will not have the same effect (the only solution would be to ensure that the fixtures and fridges are cleaned regularly). It is always wise to localize aromas to areas where they can be monitored and amended.

For years, department stores have toyed with the idea of pumping aromas through air-conditioning systems to please shoppers. This idea, however, has never been proven to work. Everyone's senses are different; what one may like, another may loathe. In an extreme case a customer may be allergic to an alien smell—with genuinely distressing consequences.

Plants

Plants are a great way of creating ambience, color, and even scent. All will need watering, but outdoor plants will need to be placed outside for periods to make them last.

Above
Fresh flowers will add character to any store. Depending on the selection and arrangement they can be either masculine or feminine. Not all flowers need to be artistically displayed in complicated arrangements with a variety of blooms. Here in New York's

Kirna Zabête, a feminine touch is added with a large collection of forsythia in a dynamic floral presentation that is neither expensive nor difficult to create.

Opposite
This rendering of the new Villa Moda store in Bahrain by Marcel Wanders aims to have all the elements that bring together the ambience of a store—theater, architecture, lighting, and mannequins.

Retail standards and maintenance, and budget

The importance of maintaining the visual standards of a store or a shop floor should never be underestimated. Enlisting the help of the sales team can dramatically affect the workload of a visual merchandiser. Training the sales staff to implement a basic level of visual merchandising that can be easily utilized will be a long-term benefit. A visual merchandiser, for example, may not require the sales associates to create displays or dress mannequins, but they can assist with the everyday merchandising of the fixtures.

Standards and maintenance

Most retailers will expect their shop floors to be neat and clean, ready for the morning trade. Producing a booklet to explain how to maintain the visual merchandising standards is an effective way of communicating the requirements to the sales associates. A generic layout can be used and then updated easily each season. Weekly training sessions conducted on the shop floor by a visual merchandiser with the sales staff will also help clarify the roles and responsibilities of staff. Giving individual ownership for specific product categories or brands will also help build a visual merchandising structure within the sales team.

Stock replenishment

Stock replenishment is best done while the store is closed, either in the evening or first thing in the morning. Managers and owners of prestigious stores do not generally allow racks and rails on the shop floor during opening hours. This discipline should be practiced in any retail environment. Customers should not be distracted by anything but the merchandise on offer.

Housekeeping

Housekeeping should also be completed while the store is shut. Walkways and aisles should be cleaned and cleared of any obstructions. Fixtures must be dusted and cleaned. Garments should be refolded or hung, remembering to ensure all the price tags are still attached. Dirty or soiled items should be either cleaned or replaced.

Cash desks

Cash desks must appear professional at all times and be uncluttered and user-friendly. Customers, especially when parting with large amounts of money, do not expect to see scribbled notes and family pictures taped to the cash register. Clean and neat flat surfaces should also be allocated for folding garments before they are placed into a shopping bag.

Budget

The budget for in-store visual merchandising also requires some thought. When ordering fixtures, the choice can be between custom-made items or those bought directly from manufacturers. The latter will often be the most economical but possibly not the most inspirational. Fixtures should, however, be seen as an investment; unlike a window scheme, they will have a longer retail life. When planning an in-store floor layout, budget money should also be set aside for additional lighting, graphics, and signage, which are often overlooked. A hard-wearing floor may also add additional costs to the overall project but, in the long term, will be cost-effective.

Virtual visual merchandising

For many years visual merchandisers have had to rely on a sheet of graph paper and a pencil to draw out their floor plans. Today, however, technology is available that makes the process of creating a floor layout or designing a store quicker and more effective. Various computer programs can be used to create a "virtual store." Used in tandem with buying and merchandising functions, these programs can hold libraries of merchandise that is, or will be, in-store at any one time. Such virtual products can be dragged and dropped onto fixtures that are also part of a separate library which the visual merchandiser can either build or import from suppliers' catalogues.

First, walls and floors are created to scale, and then custom color schemes can be added. Once the fixtures are in place, the products can be hung on rails, or folded

items can be placed on shelves or tables. The complete store design can be viewed as either a plan or an elevation, and with some programs the user can take a three-dimensional tour of the space. Lighting can also be directed to the relevant fixture and adjusted to give an even more realistic point of view. Mannequins, signage, and graphics can also be added to create in-store displays.

The computer programs are by no means inexpensive, but in the long run they can be cost-effective because of their versatility. With just a few days of professional training, and even more of practice, they can be used to produce excellent-quality visuals.

Above
A computer program by MockShop showing the overall layout of the virtual store. It offers the ability to generate a plan for each fixture, including each item's style or color, unit and location of each fixture, along with the appropriate signage.

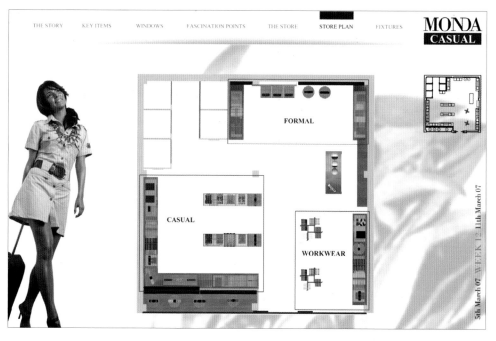

THE STORY   KEY ITEMS   WINDOWS   FASCINATION POINTS   THE STORE   **STORE PLAN**   FIXTURES

MONDA CASUAL

FORMAL

CASUAL

WORKWEAR

5th March 07   WEEK 12   11th March 07

Store communication: design directives

Worldwide, multi-chain retailers as well as the individual brands themselves continue to give importance to brand identity and want to ensure a consistent brand message and experience for the consumer in all stores. To achieve this, the visual merchandising function now extends as far as corporate headquarters, where a unified vision is created and disseminated to the stores in the form of design directives.

Directives generally follow either a vertical or horizontal path. Retailers like Gap create design directives at the corporate level. These highlight key seasonal trends and include: window displays; trend area displays found immediately inside the store entrance, featuring the latest trends of the season; departmental displays that focus on the consumer end-use; and floor plans for an A—B—C store-level hierarchy, where A stores do the highest volume of sales and carry the full collection, and other stores do less volume and carry limited groups from the collection. Directives are sent to individual shops (the process is known as vertical dissemination), where staff are relied upon to carry out the directives in each outlet. District and regional managers frequently visit these stores to make sure directives are correctly implemented in a timely manner.

Brands often supply retailers with branded fixtures to create in-department branded areas. Regardless of whether they provide branded fixtures, however, vendors also create directives containing information about seasonal advertising, trends, and collections, with suggestions for merchandise placement. Some vendors may rely on store staff to implement these directives (horizontal dissemination).

Many retailers and brands are investing in proprietary trade software to integrate their merchandise management and streamline their operations. The value of these programs is that they allow designers, merchandisers, and retailers to work and communicate visually. This is a great advantage, since 90 per cent of all information input is visual.

U.S. brands such as Levi's, Calvin Klein, Tommy Hilfiger, and Dockers, and retailers such as Macy's and Dillard's have chosen British-based Visual Retailing to provide an integrated suite of software programs that includes storyboarding, assortment planning, analysis, collection building, database management, and fixture design as well as visual merchandising in the form of VisualStore, also known as MockShop.

Above
MockShop allows the visual merchandiser to create a floor plan for the store, either digitally or via hard copy, to communicate the design directives.

The virtual store

The retail outlet is modeled in three dimensions, with all the components of the brand image and collection represented. The physical shop materials selection (i.e. floor materials, paint colors, etc.), windows, signature or branded fixtures, in-store signage, as well as merchandise are combined in three-dimensional views for ease of merchandising at retail level. When a retailer elects to use Visual Retailing, VR representatives work with the company to build a variety of "libraries": fixtures, store decor, and interior materials (flooring, paint, etc.). The retailer enters its items, signage, and mannequins into a seasonal database.

Using drag-and-drop technology and a series of libraries, visual merchandisers can determine the size and configuration of the space and assign flooring, wall, and ceiling coverings. Working in a combination of plan and 3-D views, they drag and drop fixtures from a library and arrange them on the selling floor. Each fixture contains a "connector," a "container," or a combination of the two, which allows merchandise to be placed on the fixture. Connectors place hanging items on fixture bars and arms, while containers automatically fold garments on shelving or flat surfaces, or accept graphics. Merchandise can be moved from hanging to folded areas or vice versa, and the program displays them in the correct mode. The number of units assigned to each arm, bar, or shelf can be increased or decreased.

Once the floor merchandising is complete, the visual merchandiser can then prepare images of various views of the store and fixtures for use in the design directive. An individual fixture plan that details the items and their placement can be generated as well. Finally, an overall statistics report for the floor plan can be created, detailing item information and retail value in a spreadsheet format, with a final calculation of projected sales per square or linear foot.

Directives can be created in the "visual storyboard:" a page-layout tool which is useful for creating mood, inspiration, and collection development communications as well. As information is updated and changed in any area of merchandising—for example, changing a color or style—the updates are

automatically reflected throughout. Because of its visual approach, visual retailing is easy to use once you master the icons, shortcuts, and processes necessary to complete the tasks.

Design directives are generated several times each year to coincide with seasonal collections and delivery. For example, fashion apparel often includes autumn, spring, vacation, and transitional seasons. Design directives would be generated for each of these aspects.

Design directives are seasonal design guides which include some or all of the following information:

Overall seasonal trend information, advertising, fixtures, other general miscellaneous information.

- -

An overview of how the merchandise category works across collections or classifications (i.e. shoes, lingerie, etc.).

- -

In-depth information by collection or classification, such as a possible "theme," key color, textures, fabrics or styles, display ideas, fixture flow and categories, and floor plans, and any other notes specific to the merchandise category.

Above
Further features of the MockShop program offer visual storyboards for key items (top), windows (middle), and fixtures (bottom).

Store study:
Giorgio Armani

Giorgio Armani's Hong Kong store boasts not only two floors of fashion but also an awe-inspiring shopping experience. An Armani store opening anywhere in the world will cause a predictably high level of publicity and media attention. With this in mind, and with the confirmed success of his other stores, Armani unquestionably did not stint on the design of his first Oriental shopping emporium.

Concept

The brainchild of Doriana D. Mandrelli and Massimilano Fuksas, the contemporary concept was developed around fluidity. The use of a red fiberglass ribbon emerging from the floor and then weaving its way across and through the floor acts as a tool to help customers steer their way through the café space and proves useful as a bar, dining table, and DJ stand. This witty yet inspiring design is not meant to be understated.

Architecture

In the main shopping space, blue resin floors support curved glass showcases, satin-steel furniture, and other merchandise fixtures. Every detail has been thought through carefully, with great attention given to detail and finish.

Above
A mixture of hanging rails and shelves is used to display products. Care has been taken to ensure that the top shelf and the rails are all at the same height, creating a strong focal area within the department. Products displayed on the shelves have a generous allowance of surrounding space, and each pile is limited to just two of each item, reinforcing the exclusivity of the merchandise. There is also a generous, even amount of space between the hangers. Note how the rows of black garments are highlighted with neutrals, presenting a strong fashion look.

Below
The focal and talking and meeting point of the Armani shop is the red lacquered bar that weaves its way through the dining area. It is an impressive, eye-catching piece of shop fitting that reinforces the contemporary design of the store.

Although the interior may have been designed with the product in mind in terms of designated fixtures, for the visual merchandiser it is still challenging. There are many stores that are being created today that rely heavily on contemporary design to promote their brands with the use of dynamic fixtures and open spaces. The challenge for the visual merchandiser and architects is to ensure the product should have empathy with the overall design theme and not be overshadowed. Getting the correct balance between design and merchandise is essential.

Fixtures

Every fixture has been considered not only for its design value but also for its practicality. For the Armani store, as for any new store project, the fixtures have been designed specifically for the relevant product areas as they were planned at the store-design stage; because of this early planning, they are an integral part of the store's architecture and do not stand out as an afterthought. Designing a fixture without this attention to detail can be detrimental to the overall appearance of the store and will incur an unnecessary cost if they have to be redesigned and manufactured afresh.

How many fixtures are eventually housed in their host department will of course depend on the quantity of merchandise they are to carry. In the Armani outlet, they have clearly considered this when planning the store's layout, the prime consideration being the high profile and perceived exclusivity of the product, leading to a limited number of fixtures being placed in any one area to avoid compromising the brand identity.

As well as gauging how many fixtures should be used in a department, it is essential to the Armani brand to guarantee that its garments are also correctly spaced on each fixture.

Above
Co-ordinated collections of menswear are shown on two hanging rails.
The mannequin adjacent demonstrates how the look can be put together.

Hanging items

The monotony created by a succession of clothing rails can be unappealing to the eye; it can also be offputting to the customer. By hanging complete fashion looks together on only a couple of yards of rail, and by segregating them from the other themes, the buyer will be able to focus on a complete outfit and trend. Using black as a base color intersected with neutrals or a single color gives the customer a clear idea of how the individual items should be worn. The length of the garments is also instrumental in focusing attention on the fixture and the clothes it carries; Armani cleverly uses items with different lengths to add variation to the rails.

Folded items

The careful placement of products is carried onto merchandising of the shelves, too. The glass shelves that carry folded stock are by no means overcrowded; notice how the product has the appearance of exclusivity because of the number of items stacked on top of each other—in most cases, only two items are stacked in a pile. The space between each stack of folded clothing is also a clear statement of their value. To ensure that all of the items sit neatly together, a folding board has been used.

Cleverly, an example of one of the items folded on the shelves is also hung on the hanging rails adjacent to the shelves. The folded items act as back-up stock to the hanging items. Here, the piles will include various sizes, with the hanging item in the most popular size.

Mid-floor fixtures

The mid-floor fixtures not only carry more products, but they also act as interesting pieces of furniture that are used to break up the space as well as adding another product-dressing element. Here the fixtures carry just a few items from the surrounding area. The items pulled together show a cross-section of the clothing available and the relevant co-ordinating accessories.

Mixed product categories

Although a store such as Armani specializes in fashion items that are usually promoted on hanging rails and shelves, the shop floor also carries other fixtures housing other products that will help to vary the pace of the store's layout. Here, the idea of selling books in what is predominantly a fashion store helps generate sales but, more importantly, creates a unique shop-within-a-shop to help draw customers into the store. Selecting books that are relevant to the Armani customer and displaying them in an area near an entrance is done to attract shoppers who may not necessarily be regular Armani customers, but who may wish to buy into the Armani lifestyle.

In-store display

The mannequins used to display the Armani clothing have been designed with the store's contemporary theme in mind. Their clear fiberglass heads and torsos are sympathetic to the surrounding glass fixtures and walls and by no means overshadow the interior design or the clothing. Their ghostly presence is subtle, yet effective. With the mannequins immaculately dressed in items that are hanging or folded adjacent to them, they act not only as an inspirational tool to inform the customers of the trend but also as an informative guide, showing how the clothes can be worn. Instead of grouping these mannequins, elevating them on a base and creating a focused display, they have been located in designated areas throughout the store to create focal points, allowing the customer to pause, take in the product available in-store, and look around.

Above
An elongated mid-floor fixture does not look out of place with the wall fixtures and overall store design. It can be used for flat product presentations or left empty, simply to divide the space.

Graphics and signage

A brand such as Armani relies on the architecture and store design to promote the brand, and because of this, signage does not need to be bold and overstated. Here, the brand does not need to be promoted with text; the architecture and product will prove sufficient.

There are, however, areas where graphics can be used in a particularly striking way. In the cosmetics area, the use of large graphics encompasses the brand identity: bold, colorful, and striking. Set back from the windows the graphics act as a powerful window display and an informative device. In a cosmetics department that is mostly neutral in tone, their dramatic color is used to enforce the vibrant cosmetics displayed there.

Lighting

Using lighting to illuminate the walls behind both the hanging and folded clothing is an effective backdrop that will not only highlight the product but also help guide the customers to it. The frosted glass panels help to diffuse the light, providing an even glow. Spotlights, used for highlighting alone, have been sunk into the ceiling and have adjustable fittings that are directed at the merchandise.

Like the Armani stores in Shanghai and the first Armani emporium in Milan, the Hong Kong store is an eye-catching and inspirational shopper's paradise. The layout and merchandising of the fixtures, along with the store design, are truly motivating. The complete store concept fuses Italian chic with Oriental grace.

Above
Three shelves placed at eye level are used to present the books face-out. This is an excellent idea for a bookshop carrying an edited selection of books.

Below
Strong, powerful graphics give the beauty area a completely different look to the apparel departments, introducing an area of color in an otherwise neutral store.

Mannequins

"Mannequins are very much in vogue today. Fashion is not just about the clothes anymore; it's about the hair and make-up, too—the complete look. What better tool than a good mannequin to get a fashion statement across to the masses? There was a trend in the eighties to try and use other props to carry clothes; garments were hung on broom handles; headless torsos and blow-ups of artwork were all tried but were not necessarily as successful."

Kevin Arpino, Creative Director, Adel Rootstein Display Mannequins

Mannequins have been the trademarks of window displays for decades. They are the most effective tools you can use to present the latest fashion trends. Some customers aspire to look like them and visual merchandisers often form a friendship with them. Many individuals still do not realize that these fiberglass showroom dummies are in fact modeled on actual people.

Adel Rootstein Mannequins is the world-renowned manufacturer of mannequins. With two new collections added to its vast range every year, its mannequins are bought and used by retailers worldwide. Adel began her career in 1956, making wigs and supplying display props to the retail trade from her kitchen in London. Being aware of the growing social and fashion trends of the early 1960s, she began creating models of London's style icons. Her first major mannequin was a cast of the sixties' fashion model Twiggy. Later models included Jodi Kid, Joan Collins, Sandie Shaw, Joanna Lumley, Karen Mulder, and Yasmin Le Bon, to name but a few. Her legacy lives on, and today's visual merchandisers trust

her mannequins to help realize their creative displays.

Kevin Arpino has been fundamental in driving Adel's business empire. As creative director, he is responsible for selecting whom to immortalize as a mannequin, building collections and dressing them in his legendary unique style for the many Rootstein showrooms worldwide.

Although mannequins have been fundamental to window displays in stores globally, it is worth noting that mannequins have not always been so fashionable. As Kevin Arpino explains, "In the fifteenth century, mannequins were made to represent the Madonna; they were carried through the streets of Europe as part of religious festivals. In a way, even then they were designed to carry clothes. The early Madonnas were made from papier mâché and leather and were very primitive-looking. The French can be credited for refining the mannequin. In the 1800s, the Parisian House of Worth produced mannequins that were an extension of the forms used for making clothes. Often they were used to emphasize the trend of the day and they had nipped-in waists to show corsets and bustiers.

"The mannequins of the twenties looked more contemporary because they were fashioned in the style of the period: Art Deco. Fashion designers were keen to show their creations on a torso that was 'of the moment.' Adel should really be credited for introducing commercial mannequins that were fashion-forward and inspiring. She was very aware of the growing ready-to-wear collections that had a higher turnover than the couture costumes. Mannequins needed to look younger; the mannequins before the swinging sixties resembled someone's mom!"

Above
Grouping mannequins is a skill that takes a long time to master. Deciding which two work together and how they should be positioned often depends on the strength of the outfits and their poses.

Opposite
These mannequins are part of a range that are designed to interact with each other. Although not easy to dress or group, they can be used to create more provocative displays.

Sculpting

A mannequin begins as a clay sculpture; most mannequins are modeled on real people. At Rootstein the model sits for the sculptor for a two-hour sitting every day for three weeks. The sculpting is done in the traditional way by placing the wet clay onto a wire armature. The hands are the only part of the body that is cast from life. Once the sculpture is finished, the clay figure is cast in plaster. The plaster then becomes the mold for the fiberglass mannequin that is sent off to the stores. The whole process takes three months from start to finish.

Creating a range of mannequins is time-consuming. Each model must have an individual pose that will sit within the complete collection. On occasion, a model will come to a casting and the whole collection will change because of that. Erin O'Connor, for example, had such a strong idea of how she saw herself

working as a mannequin that Rootstein changed and adapted the collection to suit her style.

As a popular and successful company, Rootstein constantly needs to update its collections. As Kevin Arpino explains, "I start putting ranges together by ascertaining what we and the customer require. During the eighties, for example, many stores were ripping out their windows to give the customer a view of the store. Mannequins that had once been viewed through a sheet of glass were then suddenly scrutinized by customers in-store; the hair and make-up needed to be refined. Retailers also saw the potential of using mannequin forms in-store to promote their merchandise; headless forms painted white were used against sparse white walls so that the clothes stood out, and the mannequins became part of the design and architecture of the store. The dramatically posed and dressed models stayed in the windows.

"We also have to take into consideration the nature of the retailers' business. If they have a boutique selling couture, they might require a dramatic, elegant pose that suits the product they are showing. Retailers in busy shopping areas may require a more simplistic pose, and sports shops might prefer an action mannequin. It is also important to remember that not everyone has the skill to dress a mannequin with a striking pose; often the Saturday girl with no experience will be challenged with the task of dressing the windows—a simple collection with no striking poses that are difficult to dress will always be beneficial. We have around 500 different mannequins in our range, many of which belong to collections. A collection is generally made up of 12 models that are designed to interact with each other if used well."

Above
Model Yasmin Le Bon sits for Adel Rootstein's sculptor. After many sittings, the mannequin is then cast and the features will be lifelike.

Below
Erin O'Connor's strong personal style influenced the collection Rootstein created using her as a model.

Opposite
A finished mannequin is posed with the model on whom it is based. The body will be exactly to scale and the features almost identical.

Purchasing mannequins

Purchasing a selection of mannequins for a store will provide a range of options to help promote any fashion collection. Whether just one or a whole collection is required, consideration should be given to what they will be used for, where they will be used, and if their poses will be suitable for the clothing they will be wearing. Remember: a sports-inspired mannequin may not be suitable for an eveningwear collection.

Mannequins come in all shapes and sizes: from adults to children, maternity to action, and stylized to realistic. Before purchasing a range of mannequins, consider the type of business in which they are to be used. A commercial, easy-to-dress range of mannequins which have simple poses will give more flexibility and will adapt to the ever-changing fashion trends. A dramatically posed mannequin may work well in a heavily stylized environment.

A range should be selected carefully so that the mannequins can be used individually or grouped to create a family; this might include a selection of standing, sitting, lying, and leaning mannequins. Yet it is worth thinking about whether or not you need more dramatic poses; do remember, though, that an expensive mannequin designed for hanging many be used in one scheme but will not be used throughout the rest of the year. An extreme pose may also be difficult to dress.

At the same time, consider how long the range will last. A dramatically posed, realistic mannequin can easily be used to promote a fashion-forward look with the right hairstyle and makeup, which can then be re-styled from season to season. It is worth bearing this in mind if you are working to a tight budget—you may not need to purchase new mannequins if you can reuse existing ones. You can, of course, also save by purchasing some styles

of mannequin that can be used time and time again for one style of garment: a rigid bust form, for example, for a man's suit. An economical range could also be built up from mannequins with no facial features, or even no heads, because they do not require makeup renovations or wigs.

Having said all this, many retailers still prefer just a simple bust form that resembles a torso and will carry clothing without overpowering the garment. These are most suited to men's tailors and classic women's fashion stores where, traditionally, stylized mannequins are not used.

The quantity of mannequins you purchase may be costly, but do consider how many are required to create a complete window fashion scheme. Ten windows with three mannequins in each will equate to 30. The interior display sites will require even more, thus adding to the mannequin budget. A range of children's mannequins, on the other hand, will not necessarily fill a large window because of their size. They will inevitably work better as a large group, and this should be borne in mind if you are working in a children's store.

Another consideration to be borne in mind is that renovating mannequins can take up to a month; it may be worth having a secondary collection to use while they are out of service, especially if your store only retails fashion. Clearly, while the mannequins are away being renovated, this would be a good time for a department store to install a home-related scheme.

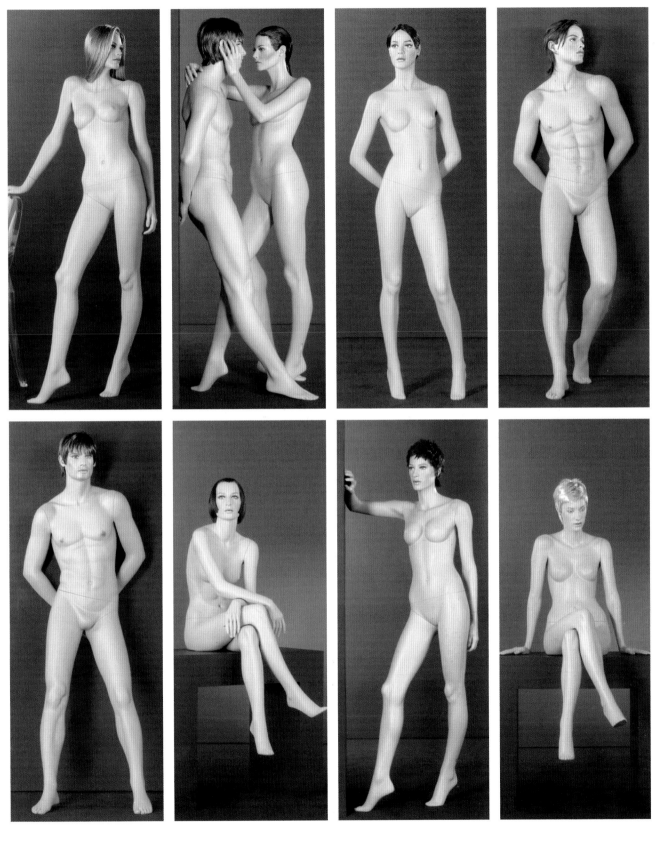

Above

A range of mannequins is designed so that they interact with each other. The majority will be standing, but sitting, lying, and leaning mannequins are also introduced to break the pace and add interest. Customers can buy complete ranges or individual.

Dressing a mannequin

"A mannequin can be a great prop for a display; if dressed badly, however, they can look awful. People do the strangest things to mannequins that they just would not do to themselves. If a dresser is unsure of how to dress the mannequin, [he or she] should keep it simple. Clothes should be given movement; if the model's hands are on the hip, throw the coat over it—don't just let it hang. Pinning a garment is paramount not only to ensure the clothes fit, but also that they look good. A pin should never be seen—a good dresser will pin the inside of the garment. Realistically, a size-14 dress should be pinned so well that it looks great on a size-10 mannequin. When I dress a showroom with over 40 models, I always dress one first of all from head to toe to make certain that I will be happy with the look I am trying to achieve."

Kevin Arpino, Creative Director, Adel Rootstein Display Mannequins

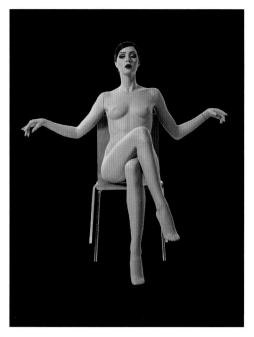

Dressing a mannequin is not as easy as it appears. Apart from having to disassemble them, they can be very heavy and clumsy, depending on the pose. The end result should, however, look as elegant and as lifelike as possible.

The dressing of men's and women's mannequins can differ; consequently the guidelines on page 191 cover both categories. Children's mannequins should also be categorized by their gender when being dressed. Once you have decided which mannequins are to be used, it is essential to follow these guidelines.

Above
A sitting mannequin with a strong pose that will look effective as part of a display, but is difficult to dress if she is to wear pants because her legs are crossed. Rather than remove a leg, loosen it slightly and pull pants up and over the knee to the waist.

Above
To create movement on these
mannequins riding horses in a Harvey
Nichols window, London, the skirt
hems and other materials have been
wired through the seam and molded to
give a lifelike appearance.

Above
Before it is dressed, a mannequin can be broken into sections. The hands, arms, waist, and one leg from this mannequin are detachable to help dressing. Skilled dressers may not need to disassemble the mannequin completely but loosen some joints.

Below
Once dressed, the same mannequin takes on a completely different appearance.

Dressing menswear

All clothing should be pressed and steamed beforehand.

Both mannequin legs should be secured together and turned upside down, resting on the floor so that the feet are facing upwards. At this stage socks should be placed on the feet and pants pulled over and down to the waist, ensuring that they remain taut to prevent creasing. Most tailored pants are unfinished and should be measured, turned up, and pinned prior to dressing. Shoes can now be added.

The clothed legs can now be returned to the upright position, and the torso can be fitted back onto the legs.

The upper garments can now be placed around the torso or pulled over the head onto the body. At this point, shirtsleeves should be pulled through the jacket arms, ready for the manne-quin's arms to be fitted.

To fit the arms, remove the hands and carefully push an arm through the layers of clothing down the

sleeves toward the cuff. Then secure the arm to the socket on the torso.

The hands can now be reattached to the arms and the mannequin can be placed in its final position.

Now is the time to dress the mannequin properly. Start by ensuring that the pants are the correct length. Tuck shirts carefully into the pants.

Loose-fitting garments can now be carefully gathered at the rear of the mannequin, or at the point that is least visible to the public. The excess fabric should be folded inwards and pinned, preferably through the seams to limit any damage to the garment.

The mannequin can now be styled and accessorized, paying attention to detail and finish.

Finally, it is always advisable to view the mannequin from the same direction as the public. Check for visible pins, loose threads, and ill-fitting clothes.

Dressing womenswear

As with menswear, it is essential that all clothing is pressed and steamed beforehand.

The legs should be assembled and turned upside down. If hosiery is required, it should be added at this stage by carefully rolling down and over the legs.

Pants and shoes should be treated in the same way as for menswear.

Unlike male mannequins, female mannequins will often have different-sized insteps. A mannequin with a high instep will require the exact heel height to ensure that it stands upright, while those with no instep will need flat shoes such as a pump.

The mannequin can now be turned upright and should be secured in its final position.

To fit a skirt or dress, turn the legs back into the upright position and attach the torso. On most occasions the garment can now be pulled over the head and secured in place, but

often a tight-fitting skirt will have to be pulled over the feet and up to the torso before the shoes are fitted and the mannequin is turned upright.

Top garments can be added and arms attached as for menswear.

Styling and accessorizing can now be completed. This should include pinning, draping, and pleating the garment to create an inspirational silhouette.

To begin, take the mannequin to the place where it will be displayed. This should be done with care because mannequins are fragile. Most new mannequins—or newly renovated ones—will be delivered with their limbs and body parts packaged separately. It is best to ensure that you have all the correct body parts before attempting to construct the mannequin. Remember: the limbs from one mannequin are not compatible with another. Many mannequins come with markings on their body parts so that they can be easily matched to the torso, thus making the assembly effortless.

If your mannequin has been in storage, it may need to be cleaned with a light detergent to remove any dust. Attention should be given to the face in particular as this is the area that is most visible. It is sometimes advisable that two people dress a mannequin if it has a complicated pose, one visual merchandiser to support the mannequin while the other dresses it.

"The visual merchandisers at Bergdorf Goodman in New York know exactly how to dress a mannequin, as do those at Neiman Marcus. Both have very skilled dressers that prove how mannequins can add drama to a window display. Zara uses mannequins very well. They realize how they can help sell their product."

Kevin Arpino, Creative Director, Adel Rootstein Display Mannequins

Advanced styling for mens- and womenswear

Many experienced visual merchandisers will not stop at using outlandish wigs, makeup, and styling. Occasionally they will wire hemlines invisibly to give the garment movement, apply hand-painted acrylic nails to the mannequin's hands, and cut and style wigs to suit the overall look. This advanced styling is best noted at prestigious department stores such as Barneys in New York and Harrods in London.

Rachel Sproule has been dressing mannequins since the age of 17 when she took a job as a junior dresser at London's Harvey Nichols store. Since then, she has taught her skills to various visual merchandising teams at Selfridges and New Look, showing the dedication to mannequin dressing which made her a leader in the U.K.'s visual merchandising fashion circuit. She continues to share her knowledge at London's fashion retail academy where she lectures. Her tips are:

Tape tissue paper to the legs of a mannequin to give volume and movement to a skirt.

Push a couple of pins through the lapel or breast of your shirt/sweater so that you can get access to them easily when pinning a mannequin's clothing.

Shoes can be slid over the feet of a mannequin that has already been set in the rod by easing the weight of the mannequin up but not completely off the rod. Turn the shoes sideways and slip them on, then lower the mannequin back onto the rod again.

Cushioned wig tape can be applied to the mannequin's head at the front and the sides to help support a heavy wig. Pins can be pushed through the wig and secured into the tape.

If you need to twist the arm of a mannequin from its natural position to hold a handbag, place a large bangle around the mannequin's wrist to disguise the unaligned join.

If a mannequin has not got pierced ears, temporary adhesive can be used to secure clip-on earrings.

Double-sided tape can be used to secure stockings to the legs of mannequins.

If a belt is too large for a mannequin, shorten it to fit by wrapping an elastic band around the excess at the back of the mannequin.

Wannabe makeup artists should leave it to the experts who work on mannequins—professionally. Cosmetics will melt and run; paint will not.

Above
A simple bust form is often the best way to display men's tailoring. Here at Thomas Pink the articulated arms are moved into a position so that the hand interacts with the tie.

Securing a mannequin

There are numerous ways that a mannequin can be secured, but there are three universal fittings that are generally used to support a mannequin.

The first is the foot rod, which is a round or square metal stick attached to a base plate made from either glass or metal; the rod is pushed into the foot to support the mannequin. The rod can also be removed from the base plate and screwed directly into the floor; the downside of the foot rod is that the shoes will have to be drilled through so that the rod can go through the sole of the shoe.

To get a mannequin to stand straight and upright on a base plate, gently ease it to the tip of the rod, place your foot on the base plate to secure it, and use the mannequin's height as a lever to bend the rod to the position required. Finally lower the mannequin back onto the base plate.

The second option, the leg rod, works in the same way but goes into the calf of the leg, which means that shoes can easily be shown without damaging them. In the U.S., the last option, the butt rod, is often preferred. A longer rod is pushed through the leg of the pants or under the skirt and fits into a hole in the butt cheek.

Many skilled professionals use wire to support mannequins. This complicated technique is called "strike." Two wires are wrapped around the waist of the model and firmly secured by twisting the wire around itself, then pulled taut in two opposing directions, ensuring that the mannequin is upright and attached to the floor with nails. The wire is then twisted around itself and the excess is cut off. Once the wire and the nail head are painted the same color as the background, they become invisible.

When striking a mannequin wearing swimwear or lingerie, ensure that the model wire is secured around the fitting that holds the torso and legs together, trail the wire though the gap between the two and to the rear of the mannequin or the part of the body that will not be seen by the public. One wire should then be pulled through the legs and the other toward the back and attached to the floor, thus the wire will not be seen around the naked waist of the mannequin.

Keep a selection of Perspex or wooden blocks (which can be painted the same color as the floor) in various sizes that can be used to block (raise and support) the heel of a shoe if the mannequin has a high instep. This will also help when striking, ensuring that the mannequin is straight and balanced.

Above left
The mannequins in this window from Macy's demonstrate the use of striking. Wire is secured to the back of the waist, then pulled taut and nailed into the floor panel. Wires can then be painted out using the same-color paint as the background.

Above right
Three mannequins on an in-store display are stabilized using base plates. A metal rod is attached into the leg so that the shoes are not damaged. A foot rod would go through the sole of the shoe.

Grouping mannequins

Most mannequin ranges are designed so that they can be positioned in an aesthetically pleasing way. They are often developed to interact with each other. Badly positioned or grouped mannequins can have a detrimental effect on the overall creative effect of any display.

Grouping models is a skill that will create something that is gratifying for the customer to look at. A line of ten models may not be inspirational; it may be better if they were positioned to interact with each other. A window with six mannequins should also be broken up into groups, such as a group of three, two, and a solo figure. Ideally there should be only a couple of overstyled stars in the window; the other mannequins should support them.

Mannequins wearing pants should always be positioned behind ones wearing skirts so that they do not block the skirt; short coats should be in front of long ones. At the same time, you can take advantage of these groupings to help the customers understand the different clothes used in the window or display. A suit that comes with either a skirt or pants can be shown easily on a group of three mannequins, demonstrating all of the options, and the group can be given cohesion by carrying accent colors onto the other models.

Above
It is important that mannequins interact with each other. Even the eyes should always focus on something, such as another mannequin, to create a more lifelike appearance.

Maintenance

Mannequins should be well cared for and kept clean. A simple felt body bag can be used to cover them when they are in storage. Dirty, chipped mannequins will not help sell any clothes. Once a mannequin has been purchased it can be resprayed and have new makeup applied; in the trade this is referred to as a "reno." Kevin Arpino describes the process: "Mannequins come back to us. We start by stripping the face of the makeup. We then take off layers of the base paint, fill any cracks, and respray them. Finally, we create and apply new makeup. A full renovation face and makeup costs around $160 (£80), whereas a new mannequin would cost between $1,400 and $2,000 (£700 and £1,000).

"Wigs are also an economical way of changing the mannequin's appearance. We offer two wig options: hard and soft hair. Both options will cost between $120 and $200 (£60 and £100). A hard wig is styled and set so that it will keep its shape and not move. They can be extremely dramatic but not very versatile. Soft hair resembles a more conventional wig that can be styled by the visual merchandiser."

Mannequin dressing is an art that many take very seriously. Visual merchandisers take a lot of pride in styling their muses. Often they use their experience to leap into the fashion world as stylists. Kevin Arpino, an advocate of mannequin dressing, believes it is a dying skill that should be studied and practiced. "Those fashion dressers that aspire to dressing the world's top models for an eight-page shoot in *Vogue* should remember they are only as good as their address book," he says. "Their first job as a stylist may be to dress someone to resemble a grandma for a dishwashing-soap commercial. Styling a mannequin can be more rewarding. At least they don't question what you are putting them in."

Above
A dramatically posed mannequin supports this elaborate couture gown.

The Visual Merchandiser's Studio

To some visual merchandisers, a studio can be a luxury; to others, it is a necessity. Large established department stores have always been allocated a space, either in the flagship store or away from the retail environment, where they can plan and create their windows and in-store displays. Depending on the needs of the visual merchandiser, this valuable accommodation can include complete workshops and even dummy windows that can be used to test future window schemes and displays.

Costly to run and maintain, many of these in-house studios, unfortunately, have been converted into selling or storage space. Much of the work that they used to produce is now contracted out to props specialists. However, a visual merchandiser lucky enough to have the space and staff to run a studio will benefit from having the equipment listed below.

Office space

For organizing and designing and the storage of files and drawings.

Product preparation space

A clean and dust-free area where products can be stored before or after they go into a window. Running rails should also be installed for garments and shelves for fashion accessories.

Ironing and steaming

A professional iron and ironing board and an industrial steamer are necessities for prepping fashion items.

Workbench

This should be large enough to take a 8 x 4 ft (2.4 x 1.2 m) sheet of wood. The bench should be sturdy with a fixed wooden top.

Spray booth

A designated area should be allocated for a spray booth that has adequate ventilation; most spray paint is extremely toxic.

Sink

A large sink with hot and cold water.

Tool cabinet

A metal storage cabinet that can be locked will protect valuable tools.

Plan chest

A large plan chest is the most efficient way to store plans and visuals.

Storage

Separate storage is needed for spare light fixtures and lamps, to hold cleaning equipment, and for paints, brushes, and cleaners.

Sign-holder shelf or cupboard

Perspex sign-holders will scratch if not cared for. A designated shelf or cabinet will help keep them in good condition.

Ample electric sockets

Rather than running the risk of causing an accident by trailing extension cords across the studio, electric sockets should be housed near the areas where power tools will be used.

Industrial vacuum cleaner

A domestic cleaner will not be sufficient.

Overhead lighting
Efficient lighting that gives a good overall light.

Fans
Ventilation for both paint fumes and sawdust.

Opposite
A typical visual merchandiser's studio will consist of props, products, and space to design and prepare various displays.

The visual merchandiser's toolbox

Any visual merchandiser will benefit from having a comprehensive selection of tools. The actual toolbox should be large enough to house the tools, but not so big that it becomes a burden and takes up a vast amount of valuable window space. Windows can be confined and sometimes claustrophobic—the more compact the toolbox, the better. Items the visual merchandiser will need are listed below.

Staple gun

Probably, in conjunction with a pair of scissors, the most important tool that a visual merchandiser needs. The staple gun has many roles, including for covering floors and wall panels.

Staple remover

These small specialist tools are the only effective way of removing staples easily.

Pliers

To remove panel pins and stubborn staples.

Scissors

The trademark scissors protruding out of a back pocket often identify a visual merchandiser.

Double-sided tape

Useful for quick repairs.

Pins

As well as traditional dressmaking pins, stronger pins that are more durable and can be hammered into wooden surfaces are used. Dressmaking pins should only be used to pin garments.

Hot-glue gun

Excellent for major repairs.

Screwdrivers

Both flat-head and Phillips. An electric screwdriver is also a useful commodity for changing plugs and fuses.

Bradawl

Useful for boring holes.

Retractable tape measure

A long measure that stretches the length of a window is more effective than a shorter one.

Spirit level

Useful for ensuring any picture or graphic is level.

Wire

There are many different gauges of wire available. A selection of galvanized, florists', model, and thin wire will be sufficient.

Selection of screws and nails

A mixture of nails, including carpet tacks, panel pins, and masonry nails, will be needed for different purposes. Wood and masonry screws together with the complementary size of molly bolts will help if you are screwing into a stone or a wooden wall.

Health and Safety

Health and safety should always be taken seriously. Visual merchandisers must ensure that any public space they are working in is kept clear at all times. When working in a confined or isolated space such as a window, they must also ensure that they adhere to health and safety regulations.

> The responsibilities of a visual merchandiser may differ from day to day so take time to analyze how best to implement any health and safety rules as early as possible.

There are three areas within a store where visual merchandisers should consider both their own and the public's safety: the studio, windows, and store interiors. Listed below is a health and safety checklist for each of the areas:

Studio

Power tools should be used with the correct protective clothing: i.e. goggles and gloves when required.

Electrical apparatus should not be used near water.

Do not attempt to move heavy props by yourself; they will often require two or more people to maneuver them.

Spray paints and strong adhesives will require adequate ventilation.

Electric cables trailing across the studio floor can cause accidents.

Windows

Ensure all power tools are used with the correct protective clothing.

Many visual merchandisers prefer to dress a window without any footwear on to ensure that they do not ruin or mark the floor. Care should be taken, however, not to step on nails or staples.

Speakers connected to the store's public address system should be installed in isolated windows to keep the visual merchandiser informed of any need to evacuate the store.

Ladders should be firmly secured before use; it is advisable to have one person stabilizing the bottom while another climbs.

Lighting tracks should be earthed and wired professionally.

Never cut corners when wiring lamps, etc. Always ensure the correct fuse is used with the correct plug.

When using toxic paint, it is advisable to make sure that the window is well ventilated. It is often best to leave the window open while the paint is drying.

In-store displays

Mannequins must be secured properly: on many occasions children will want to play on them.

Ladders must only be used with another person stabilizing them. This will act as stability for the user as well as informing the customers that they are in use.

Electric cables must not trail across the shop floor at any time.

Sharp or electrical tools should never be left unattended.

Painted items must be dry before they are placed where customers will come into contact with them.

Fixtures

Any fixture used to hold merchandise must be secure and stable.

Shelves must be secured and strong enough to take the weight of the merchandise. Shelves should never be overstocked.

Any undressed fixture can be hazardous for customers; empty garment holders or arms can be dangerous. It is always advisable to remove the holder or leave at least one item of clothing on the end of the arm while re-merchandising the display to ensure that customers are aware of a potential hazard.

Lighting chart

Lamp/bulb	Voltage/fitting	Location	Suitability
Fluorescent tube lamp	High-voltage	Overhead fittings, frequently ceiling-mounted	Nondirectional; efficient; used to provide high-level overall lighting in stores
Tungsten/incandescent filament	High-voltage	Overhead lighting, table and wall fittings	Commonly used in domestic environments; often used for secondary lighting in retail outlets
Tungsten/incandescent strip light	High-voltage	Undershelf lighting, picture lights, floor lights	Nondirectional; provides a softer light output than fluorescent tubes
Tungsten, incandescent reflector lamp	High-voltage	Used with specialist fitting, in windows, in-store, and outdoor fittings	Directional light output for high-lighting specific areas of a display
Crown silver tungsten/incandescent cap lamp	High-voltage	Used with specialist fitting with adjustable reflector	Window lighting and some interior displays; can be easily focused
Halogen capsule lamp	High- or low-voltage	Window lighting and interior display. Used with specialist fitting with adjustable reflector	Highly efficient; adjustable; ideal for focal-point directional lighting for displays
Halogen dichroic lamp	Low-voltage; used with specialist fitting frequently containing a transformer	Window lighting and interior display	Sealed 1-amp for window and interior lighting, available in several beam widths. Excellent for general displays and creating theater
Metal halide lamp	High-voltage	General lighting used for window and in-store displays	Harsh, efficient strong light, low-maintenance; takes time to reach full light output capacity
Fiber optic	Low-voltage	Small display cases, effect lighting	Excellent for jewelry or similar products because the light unit can be housed remotely. Fittings are small and discreet, although with poor light output
Light-emitting diode (LED)	Low-voltage	Low light output cold-running lamp for close proximity lighting such as showcases	Poor light output. Available in several colors; unsuitable for general display lighting as it cannot be focused
Low-voltage cold cathode	Low-voltage	Similar to neon in appearance used in store signs and display effects	Available in many colors; excellent for building excitement; can be located in areas accessible to the public
High-voltage neon	High-voltage	Outside signs and effect lighting	Must be professionally installed and expensive to maintain; not suitable for interior signs

Above
This chart gives the description and the ideal uses for the various lights, available in conjunction with the correct fittings.

Opposite
Carefully positioned lights not only illuminate the area with its "Zipper" theme but are used to highlight the mannequin's face for dramatic effect.

Glossary

A

Accent lighting The use of lighting to emphasize displays or merchandise units

Adjacencies Deciding which product sits next to each other on a floor plan or layout

Ambient lighting Overall lighting used in-store

B

Balance Visual weight

Banner Printed text or graphic often suspended from the ceiling

Barriers Fixtures used to block customer flow

Base plate Metal or glass plate that houses the fixture (spigot) that supports a mannequin

Beam (lighting) The light projected from a lamp

Brand awareness Understanding the brand and its mission statement

Branding Communication tool used to enforce a designer, store, or product

Bust form Torso of a mannequin, often without a head, designed to display tops only

C

Capacity fixtures Units designed to carry fast-selling items

Ceiling grid Metal structure fixed to the ceiling of a window or interior display

Chevron Arranging fixtures at 45-degree angles to encourage customer flow

Closed window Window with a back wall

Color ways The colors manufacturers have chosen to use in their fashion of home collections

Concession Another brand bought into the host store

Cross-merchandising Pulling unconventional products together to create a display or trend area

Customer flow Maneuvering the customers through the store with ease

D

Display base Raised platform used in-store to create display on

Diwali Indian festival of light

Dressing Styling a window, grouping, or mannequin

F

Face-outs Fixture components used to show the full front of fashion items

Fixture density How much a stock a fixture will or should hold

Flagship The main store of a large retail company

Focal points Areas that stand out

Folding board Cut piece of wood or cardboard used as a template when folding clothing

Footfall Amount of customers entering a store or department

G

Gobo Design burned out of metal that light is beamed through to create a logo or design that is projected onto a surface

Gondola A four-sided fixture used primarily for home or food products

Graphic Printed picture used often as a backdrop to a display

Gridwall Metal wire wall fixture system

Grouping Product displayed to create interest

H

Hang tag Price or informative ticket attached to the product, often with a kimble gun or string, ribbon, etc.

K

Kimble gun Tool used to fix price tags to a garment

L

Layout Placing and arranging products and product categories on the retail floor

Light box Back-lit box that houses a transparency

Linear Retail wall space

Logo Name of brand used to enhance display

Luxury retailer Designer brand

M

Merchandise Product on sale

Mid-floor fixture Product fixture that is placed away from the wall, should be shopped from 360 degrees

Multiple sales Encouraging the customer to purchase more than one item

O

Open-back window Window without a back to it

Optical weight How products used in a display visually balance

P

Prepping Preparing products before hand for a display

Props Items used to enhance a display as part of a theme or scheme

R

Reno Renovation of a mannequin

Rod Metal pole that supports a mannequin either through the foot, ankle, or backside

S

Scheme The overall idea and concept of the display

Shadow box Miniature enclosed window used for smaller displays

Shop fitting Design and construction of the interior of a store

Sight-lines Use of fixtures to draw the eyes' attention

Signage All forms of tagging or text used in-store or in windows

Slatwall Slatted panels that attach to a linear wall that supports rails, shelves, and brackets to hold merchandise

Striking Use of wire to support a mannequin

T

Text Written words used on a sign

Theater Creating excitement within the retail environment

Theme The use of a creative window scheme running through the windows to create a story

Trend area Area used to display promotional or themed merchandise

V

VM Abbreviation of Visual Merchandising

W

Wall fixture System used on a retail wall to hold various fittings

Further reading

Books

New Retail
by Raul A. Barreneche
(London: Phaidon, 2005)

*Silent Selling: Best Practices and
Effective Strategies in Visual
Merchandising*
by Judith Bell and Kate Ternus
(New York: Fairchild, 2002)

*Big Ideas for Small Retailers
Discover New Ways to Improve Your
Business* (Paperback)
by John Castell
(Cirencester, Gloucestershire:
Management Books 2000, 2006)

Collidoscope: New Interior Design
by Nigel Coates
(London: Laurence King, 2004)

Store Window Design
by Aurora Cuito (ed)
(New York: TeNeues, 2005)

Fashion Retail
by E. Curtis
(New York: Wiley Academic, 2004)

*Contemporary Visual Merchandising
and Environmental Design* (5th edition)
by Jay Diamond and Ellen Diamond
(Upper Saddle River, New Jersey:
Prentice Hall, 2006)

Retail Buying (8th edition)
by Jay Diamond and Gerald Pintel
(Upper Saddle River, New Jersey:
Prentice Hall, 2008)

New Retail
by Rasshied Din
(London: Conran Octopus, 2000)

*Smart Retail: How to Turn Your
Store into a Sales Phenomenon*
by Richard Hammond
(Upper Saddle River, New Jersey:
Prentice Hall, 2003)

*Design for Shopping:
New Retail Interiors*
by Sarah Manuelli
(London: Laurence King, 2006)

Applied Visual Merchandising
by Kenneth H. Mills, Judith E. Paul and
Kay Moormann
(Englewood Cliffs, New Jersey:
Prentice Hall, 1982)

*Wonderwall: Masamichi Katayama,
Projects*
by Shigekazu Ohno
(Amsterdam: Frame and Basel:
Birkhauser, 2003)

*Visual Merchandising and Display:
The Business of Presentation*
by Martin M Pegler
(New York: Fairchild, 1983)

*Powershop: New Japanese
Retail Design*
by Carolien van Tilburg
(Basel: Birkhauser, 2002)

*Retail Success: Increase Sales,
Maximize Profits, and Wow Your
Customers in the Most Competitive
Marketplace in History*
by George Whalin
(San Marcos, California: Willoughby
Press, 2001)

Magazines

Creative Review

Frame

FX

VMSD

Websites

www.rootstein.com
Mannequin suppliers

www.patinav.com
Mannequin suppliers

www.hindsgaul.com
Mannequin suppliers

www.bonaveri.com
Mannequin suppliers

www.proportionlondon.com
Mannequin suppliers

www.universaldisplay.co.uk
Mannequin suppliers

www.morplan.com
Store equipment supplier

www.shopfittingsupplies.co.uk
Shop equipment supplier

www.fashionwindows.com
Online fashion and window information

www.elemental.co.uk
Props and visual merchandising
solutions

www.superfuture.com
Worldwide stores

www.visualretailing.com
Virtual visual merchandising

www.lectra.com
Virtual visual merchandising

Index

Page numbers in *italics* refer to illustration captions.

A
add-on sales 158, *159*
Adel Rootstein Mannequins *6, 169, 180–1,* 182, *184, 187, 188, 190, 192, 194, 195*
adjacencies 112, *113,* 204
Alexander McQueen, Milan *30,*
Alexander McQueen, New York *141*
ambience 170
anatomical merchandising 146, *146*
Armani, Giorgio *see Giorgio Armani*
Arpino, Kevin 182, 184, 188, 195
Atelier 1, Kiev *124,* 124–5, *125*

B
backlit transparencies *166,* 167, *167*
Banchet, Franck 50
banners 163, 204
Barneys, New York 50, 74, *156*
Bathing Ape, A, Japan 34
Belstaff, London *122*
Benetton, Moscow *167*
Bergdorf Goodman, New York 62
Bisazza, Berlin *28–9*
Bon Marché, Paris *11,* 13
branded shop fixtures 132
Briggs, Mark 20, 21
bronze areas *116,* 117
budgeting 61, 103, 172
bust forms *27, 192,* 204

C
cabinets 130
CAD (computer-aided design) 68, 69, *69*
capacity fixtures 204
capacity rails 136, *136*
carpenters 22
cash desks 112, 122, 172
ceiling grids 47, 204
chain stores 24, 56, 110, 174–5
checkered merchandising 146, *146*
chevroning 118, *118, 119,* 204
Christmas 60, *60,* 61, *75, 76, 98, 99,* 100, *100,* 101, *101,* 157
clearance merchandise 160
Colette, Paris *27,* 74, *128, 153*
color
    basic principles 78–83
    effect on lighting 90

sequence for hanging rails 137
    and window display themes 58
color blocking 142, *142, 143*
concept shop fits 132
concessions 132, 204
co-ordinated merchandising 147, *147*
Corso Como, Milan 34, *34, 114*
Cotungo, Joe 6
cross-merchandising 204
customer flow 204

D
Dixon, Tom 34
Dover Street Market, London 74, *130, 137, 147*
dressers 21, 22

E
Energie store, London *170*

F
fabric, covering boards with 86–7
face-outs 204
Farrar-Hockley, Rebecca 36–9
Flight 101 *148,* 148–9, *149*
floor layouts 114–22
floor panels 47
flowers, fresh 66, *66,* 102, 134, *170*
focal points *70,* 70–1, 73, *73,* 118, 204
folding boards 150, *150,* 204
Foley, David 124–5
footfalls 118, 204
Fortnum & Mason, London *66, 98, 104,* 104–7, *105, 106, 107*
found objects 126, 130, *130,* 131
freelancers 26, 101
French Connection, London *73,* 96

G
Gap 24, 174
Gerhardt, John 20, 110, 154
Giorgio Armani, Hong Kong *176,* 176–9, *177, 178, 179*
Globus Food Hall, Zurich *152*
gobos 204
gold areas *116,* 117
gondolas 126, *126,* 128, 204
graphic designers 22
graphics 50, *51, 54,* 92, 96, *96, 165,* 165–7, *166, 167, 179,* 204
gridwalls 138, 204

H
Habitat 14, 34, *34, 126*
hanging rails 136–7, 138
Harrods, London 20, 21, 30, *111*
Harvey Nichols, London *8–9, 10,* 11, 14, *46,* 50, *54, 55, 60, 72, 89, 90, 91, 99, 100, 189*
Heal's, London *163*
health and safety 201
Hewson, Linda 103
Holt Renfrew, Toronto *94*
horizontal merchandising 142, *143, 153*

I
IKEA 114
Ingram, Bartley 74–7

K
kimble guns 164, *164,* 204
Kirna Zabête, New York *163, 170*
Kurt Geiger, London *36,* 36–9, *38, 39*

L
LaChapelle, David *53*
l.a.Eyeworks, Los Angeles *135*
Lane Crawford, Hong Kong *18, 21,* 74, 74–7, *75, 76, 77, 101, 111, 155, 156, 161, 165, 166*
Liberty's, London 14, *64, 86*
lighting
    chart 202
    in-store displays 168, *168*
    mannequins *169*
    shelves 141
    window displays 48, *87,* 88, 90, *91,* 102, 107
linears 120, 204 *see also wall fixtures*

M
Macy's, New York 13, 15, 54, *64, 85, 88, 193*
maintenance of displays 102, 107, 156, 172
Maison Baccarat, Paris 32, *32, 131*
Mandarina Duck, London *56*
mannequins *6,* 182–6
    dressing *188,* 188–92, *189, 190*
    grouping *182,* 194, *194*
    lighting *169*
    maintenance 195
    purchasing 77, 186, *187*
    securing 193

Marks & Spencer 31, *164*
 Milton Keynes store *114*, *142*, *157*, *158*
Marshall Field's, Chicago 13, *13*
Max Studio, Los Angeles *46*
McCartney, Stella *see Stella McCartney*
McQueen, Alexander *see Alexander McQueen*
Miss Sixty, Barcelona *139*, *141*
MockShop *173*, 174, *174*, *175*
multiple sales 204
music 170

O
optical balance 71, *71*, 204
optical weight 204

P
painters 22
Peter Jones, London *164*
plants *60*, 66, *66*, 102, 170
platinum areas *116*, 117
point of purchase 158
positioning products 121
Prada *30*, *34*, *161*
prepping 84, 150–2, 204
Pret à Manger, London *159*
price points 204
price tags 88, 92, 95, 151, 164
Printemps, Paris *13*, *14*, 15, *47*, *51*, *62*, *78*, *83*
product blocking 144, *145*
product collections 147
props 50, 62–6, 204
pyramid groupings *68*, 69, *70*, 72, *72*

Q
Quant, Mary *12*, 14

R
reno (mannequins) 195, 204
repetition grouping 73, *73*
role of visual merchandisers 18–19, 22
Rootstein, Adel *see Adel Rootstein*

S
Safeway, California *163*
Saks, New York *87*, *92*
scents 170
schemes 54, 204
Selfridges, Birmingham 31, *31*

Selfridges, London *2*, *11*, 13, 15, *15*, *16–17*, *22*, *40–1*, *42*, 46, 48, 52, *52*, *53*, 54, 58, *58*, *59*, *60*, *80*, *83*, *92*, *93*, 98–100, *120*, *121*, *129*, *132*, 151, *154*, *160*, *169*, *192*, *199*, *202*
Selfridges, Manchester *135*
Selfridges, visual merchandising studio *196–7*, *198*
shelves, fixed 141, *141*
sight-lines 118, 120, 204
signage 204
 clearance merchandise 160
 in-store 161–7
 window displays 92–5, *94*
silver areas *116*, 117
slatwalls 138, 204
Sproule, Rachel 192
Starck, Philippe 32, *32*, *131*
Stella McCartney, London *122*
Stella McCartney, New York *45*
store design 30–4, 76
store guides 161, *164*
striking (mannequins) 193, *193*, 204
studios 199, *199*
success, measuring 27
Supreme, Los Angeles *133*
Symes, Paul 90, 104–7
symmetrical merchandising 144, *145*

T
tables 120, 122, 126, 129
themes 54, *56*, 56–60, *57*, *59*, *61*, 204
Thompson, Erin 151
tools 200
Topman, London *57*, *136*
Topshop, London *50*, *61*, *64*, *66*, *162*
training 20–1
trend areas 157, *157*, 204
Trust Nobody, Barcelona *26*, *108–9*, *153*

U
Uniqlo, Tokyo *97*, *142*

V
vendor fixtures 132
vertical merchandising 144, *144*
Villa Moda, Bahrain *170*
virtual stores 173–5

W
walkways *111*, *114*, 117, 120, *120*, *121*
wall fixtures 138–41, 204
Weston, Alannah 18, 42, 52, 58, 98–100, 103
window calendars 98–101
window displays 42
 designing 68–73
 installing 86–8
 maintenance 102
 planning 50–2
 prepping 84
 schemes 54, 204
 set-up 47–8, *49*
 themes 54, *56*, 56–60, *57*, *59*, *61*, 204
windows
 closed 44, *45*, 47, 64, 204
 layout of 70–3
 open-back 44, *45*, 87, 204
 size and style 44–6

Z
Zara *14*, 15, *25*, *45*, *84*

Picture credits and acknowledgements

Picture credits

The publisher would like to thank the following picture sources:

AFP/Getty Images: p166 bottom; Alexander McQueen, Milan, William Russell/Ed Reeve: p30 top; Apoc, Paris/Ronan and Erwan Bouroullec: p69 bottom; Atelier 1: pp124–5; Baccarat, Paris/Claude Weber: pp32 bottom, 33, 131; Barney's, New York: p156 bottom; Belstaff, London/Ed Reeve: p122; Bisazza, Berlin/Alberto Ferrero, www.albertoferrero.it: pp28–29; The Chicago History Museum: p13 top; Colette, Paris: pp27, 128, 153 top; © 10 Corso Como/Vanni Burkhart: pp34 right, 115; Dover Street Market, London: pp130, 137, 147; Flight 001, New York: pp148–9; Fortnum & Mason, London, visual presentation by Paul Symes: pp19, 104, 106 top; Fortnum & Mason, London, visual presentation by Paul Symes/Andrew Meredith: pp67, 98, 105, 106 bottom, 107; French Connection, Oxford Street: A/W 2006/ Andrew Meredith: pp73 top, 96; Giorgio Armani, Massimiliano Fuksas Architecture/Ramon Prat: pp176–9; Globus Food Hall, Brunner Eisenhut Gisi Arkitekten, Zurich: p152; Habitat Regent Street, London: pp35, 127; Halfords/© Pentagram, Harry Pearce: p163 bottom left; Harrods, London, Limited: p111 top; Harvey Nichols, London/Michael Taylor: pp46 top right, 54–5, 90–91, 99, 189 and 8–9, 10 bottom (window by Thomas Heatherwick); Harvey Nichols/Melvyn Vincent: pp60 bottom, 72 top, 89, 100; Heal's, London/© Pentagram, Domenic Lippa: p163 top right; Holt Renfrew, Canada/Jason Robinson,

Saw Photography: p94; Hulton Archive/Getty Images: p10 top; Kirna Zabête, New York: pp163 top left, p170; Kurt Geiger/Found Associates: pp36–9, 140; LA eyeworks/Fotoworks: p135 bottom; Lane Crawford, Hong Kong: pp18, 21, 74–7, 101, 111 bottom, 155, 156 top, 161 left, 165, 166 top; Liberty, Great Marlborough Street, London, by Maxine Groucutt, in collaboration with Laura Tarant Brown/ Andrew Meredith: p65; Liberty, London/Ed Reeve: p86; Macy's, New York/Paul Olszewski: pp54 bottom, 85, 88, 193 left; Mandarina Duck/ Marcel Wanders Studio: p56; Marks & Spencer: pp114, 142 bottom, 157, 158, 164 left; Maxstudio, Los Angeles/Fotoworks: p46 top left; Miss Sixty/Studio 63, Florence: pp139, 141; Carlo Moretti: p129 top; ND/ Roger Viollet/Getty Images: p11 top; Photo by Oleg Nikishin/Getty Images: p167; O2, Munich/Dan Pearlman: p134 right; Peter Jones, London/ © Pentagram, John MacConnell: p164 right; Prada, Los Angeles/© Phil Meech: p161 right; Prada, New York/ Armin Linke, www.arminlinke.com: p30 bottom; Prada, Tokyo/Ed Reeve: p34 left; Pret à Manger, London: pp159; Printemps Departmental Store, Paris, Eva Glele/© Francis Peyrat: pp13 bottom, 14 top, 47, 51, 63, 78, 82, 83 bottom; Prints, Singapore: p134 top left; Rootstein Display Mannequins: pp7, 169 bottom, 180–8, 190, 194–5; The Royal Borough of Kensington & Chelsea, Family & Children's Service/ John Bignell: p12; Saks, Fifth Avenue, New York: pp87, 92 left; Selfridges, Birmingham/Future Systems: p31; Selfridges, London/Andrew Meredith:

pp2, 15, 16–17, 23, 40–3, 46 bottom, 48, 52–3, 58–9, 60 top, 80, 83 top, 92 right, 93, 120–1, 129 bottom, 132, 154, 160, 169 top, 192, 196–8, 203; Selfridges, Manchester/ Andrew Meredith: p135 top; The Selfridges Archive at The History of Advertising Trust, www.hatads.org.uk: p11 bottom; Stella McCartney, London/ Ed Reeve: p123; Stella McCartney, New York/© Frank Oudeman, www. frankoudeman.com: p45 bottom; Justin Sullivan/Getty Images: p163 bottom right; Supreme, Los Angeles, Harry Allen & Associates/Hage: p133; Topman, London: pp57, 136, 193 right; Topshop, London: pp50, 61, 64 top, 66, 162; Trust Nobody, Barcelona: pp26, 108–9, 153 bottom; Undercover Lab, Tokyo/Nacasa & Partners Inc.: p32 top; Uniqlo, Tokyo/ Nacasa & Partners Inc: pp97, 142 top; Visual Retailing Software Distribution Ltd: pp173–5; VV Rouleux, www.vvrouleaux. com: p134 bottom left; Marcel Wanders Studio: p171; Zara/INDITEX S.A.: pp14 bottom, 25, 45 top, 84.

Illustrations by Majka Zylinkski.

Author's acknowledgements

My special thanks go to:
My agent – Ursula Hudson
at the London College of Fashion.
All at Laurence King Publishing – Helen Evans for commissioning this book, Anne Townley and Zoe Antoniou for their professional guidance and support. Gemma Stokes for the pictures and Majka Zylinski for the illustrations. The UK and US reviewers – Prof. Marie Aja-Herrera, Elisabeth Jacobsen, Janine Munslow, Anthony Parsons, and

in particular Anne C. Cecil, Instructor, Design & Merchandising, Westphal College of Media Arts and Design, Drexel University, for her contribution on virtual visual merchandising.
Those who taught and influenced me – Rowland Cleaver, Paul Dyson, Paul Symes, Rachel Sproule, Paul Muller, Patsy Pearce and Sue Atwood.
Those who sent me around the globe in search of retail enlightenment – Vittorio Radice Mahipat Singh, Suzie Hanlan and Susanne Tide-Frater. Today's players that push the boundaries of visual merchandising and also agreed to be interviewed – Alannah Weston, Erin Thompson and Linda Hewson at Selfridges, Kevin Arpino at Rootstein Mannequins, Rebecca Farrar Hockley at Kurt Geiger, Richard Found at Found Associates, Joe Cotugno at Bloomingdales, Franck Banchet and Eva Glélé at Printemps, John Gerhardt at Holt Renfrew, Paul Symes at Fortnum and Masons, Mark Briggs at Harrods, David Foley at Atelier 1, Brad John and John Sencion at Flight 001, Janet Wardley at Harvey Nichols and Bartley Ingram at Lane Crawford.
The following people for their support with this book – Jan Hamling at Liberty, James Thomas, James Shepherd, Trevor Corfield and Andrew Meredith – retail photographer extraordinaire! And all of my students who will be the future retail Gurus. And finally, my friends and family – Harvey Sutton and Mat Wilkinson, my parents for agreeing to let me spend two years studying a subject they never understood and probably never will, and Richard for his tolerance and constant support.